# *more* Quick & Easy

# SCRAPBOOK PAGES

**200** all new timesaving layouts you can create in one hour or less

**MEMORY MAKERS BOOKS**

Editor   Emily Curry Hitchingham

Art Director   Nick Nyffeler

Graphic Designers   Jordan Kinney, Robin Rozum

Art Acquisitions Editor   Janetta Abucejo Wieneke

Craft Editor   Jodi Amidei

Photographer   Ken Trujillo

Contributing Photographers   Brenda Martinez, Jennifer Reeves

Art Caption Writer   Nicole Cummings

Editorial Support   Karen Cain, Amy Glander, MaryJo Regier, Lydia Rueger, Dena Twinem

Contributing Memory Makers Masters   Jessie Baldwin, Valerie Barton, Joanna Bolick, Jenn Brookover,
Christine Brown, Susan Cyrus, Sheila Doherty, Jodi Heinen, Jeniece Higgins, Nicola Howard,
Diana Hudson, Julie Johnson, Kelli Noto, Shannon Taylor, Denise Tucker, Samantha Walker, Sharon Whitehead

Publisher   Rick Groth

Memory Makers® *More Quick and Easy Scrapbook Pages*

Published by Memory Makers Books, an imprint of F+W Publications, Inc.

12365 Huron Street, Suite 500, Denver, CO  80234

Phone (800) 254-9124

First edition. Printed in the United States.

09 08 07 06 05  5 4 3 2 1

Library of Congress Cataloging-in-Publication Data

More quick & easy scrapbook pages : 200 all new timesaving layouts you can create in
one hour or less.
   p. cm.
   ISBN 1-892127-56-3
   1. Photograph albums. 2. Photographs–Conservations and restoration. 3. Scrapbooks. I.
Title: More quick and easy scrapbook pages. II. Memory Makers Books.

TR465.M644 2005
745.593–dc22
                                                                                    2005041566

Distributed to trade and art markets by
F+W Publications, Inc.
4700 East Galbraith Road, Cincinnati, OH 45236
Phone (800) 289-0963
ISBN 1-892127-56-3

Distributed in Canada by Fraser Direct
100 Armstrong Avenue
Georgetown, ON, Canada  L7G 5S4
Tel: (905) 877-4411

Distributed in the U.K. and Europe by David & Charles
Brunel House, Newton Abbot, Devon, TQ12 4PU, England
Tel: (+44) 1626 323200, Fax: (+44) 1626 323319
Email: mail@davidandcharles.co.uk

Distributed in Australia by Capricorn Link
P.O. Box 704, S. Windsor NSW, 2756 Australia
Tel: (02) 4577-3555

Memory Makers Books is the home of *Memory Makers*, the scrapbook magazine dedicated to educating and
inspiring scrapbookers. To subscribe, or for more information, call (800) 366-6465.
Visit us on the Internet at www.memorymakersmagazine.com.

This book belongs to:

_____

Dedicated to those who create room in their schedules and
imaginations to make scrapbooking a part of life.

# Table of
# Contents

# Chapter 1

## 14 · *Design Sketches*

Clean and striking page designs for one- page layouts and two-page spreads. Includes examples for single and multiphoto arrangements.

# Chapter 2

## 36 · *Backgrounds*

Deceptively simple page background ideas for color blocking, layering, tearing, stitching, stamping, painting and more.

# Chapter 3

## Titles, Borders and Mats · 56

Fast and fun ideas for creating appealing titles, borders and mats using stickers, tags, stamps, premade accents, patterned paper, photos, slide mounts, ribbon and more.

# Chapter 4

## Embellishments · 80

Fantastic examples for using favorite accents in fresh new ways, such as metals, die cuts, punches, paper piecing, acrylics, ephemera, organics, notions and more.

# Chapter 5

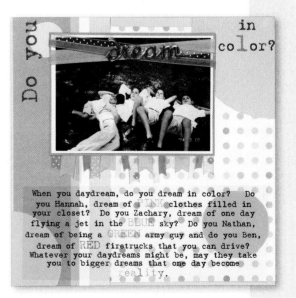

## Journaling · 108

Fail-proof formats for presenting inspired, exceptional journaling using typography, song lyrics, letters, timelines, bulleted lists, milestones, dialogue, acrostic journaling and more.

**trav·el** (trav´əl) *vi.* 〖var. of VOYAGE〗 1. to make a journey 2. to visit new places 3. an opportunity for fun, learning and growth. 〖see also LUGGAGE, SIGHT-SEEING, RECREATION〗

Just as winter weather was beginning to kick in back home in Denver, we were able to escape for a week on a Caribbean cruise. Our shore excursions brought with them some of the most incredible scenery, worthy of picture postcards, tranquil lagoons, serene beaches and lush rainforests. These photos from Belize, Cozumel and Costa Maya will serve as warm reminders of the fun we had for years to come.

# Introduction

Quick and easy—magic words that make creating artful pages in a snap possible in the whirlwind that is life. Family responsibilities, work obligations and various aspects of day-to-day living can often relegate crafting time to the bottom of our very lengthy to-do lists. With so many demands on our precious reserves of "spare" time, it has become essential to streamline, shortcut, strategize and simplify scrapbooking so that even the most abbreviated of stolen moments are minutes of crafting time well-spent.

If you're in search of straightforward but stylish pages that can be created despite your busy schedule, rest assured you needn't compromise quality or artistic merit. With *More Quick and Easy Scrapbook Pages*, we've returned with a second installment of nearly 200 all-new page ideas that can be re-created in one hour or less. Chapters chock-full of creative concepts for design sketches, backgrounds, titles, borders and mats, embellishments and journaling will leave you reeling with page ideas—and with extra time on your hands to share masterpieces no one would guess were produced in a pinch. In addition, we've compiled 20 top timesavers sure to save you hours when you've none to spare, as well as a checklist for efficient stops at the craft store to keep your scrapbook arsenal at-ready.

With the help of this comprehensive, time-friendly resource, you can easily incorporate today's latest and greatest looks without committing yourself to countless hours at the craft table. More quick and easy pages mean more time for you, more time for managing your busy life and one more thing to mark off your list of things accomplished.

Get started today!

*Emily*

Emily Curry Hitchingham, Associate Editor

# 20 Top Timesavers

## Organization

A clean, well-maintained workspace is key not only for efficient crafting; it is essential for your scrapbooking sanity. Tidying your table, throwing out waste and returning tools and supplies to their rightful places each time you create is crucial when scrapbooking against the clock. These helpful habits will put time on your side and exponentially increase your page production.

### HAVE TWO SETS OF BASIC TOOLS

Here's an instance where two is definitely better than one. Eliminate the need to constantly transfer scrapbooking essentials such as cutting mats, craft knives, rulers, paper trimmers and adhesives between your craft room and portable cropping bag by having a complete set for each. In doing so, you prevent scrapbooking standstills for lack of supplies—and unnecessary upheaval when it comes time to crop.

### SORT AND LABEL PHOTOS

Few things behoove you more than taking a minute to group and categorize your photos immediately after having them developed. Sort photos by occasion, date, theme, or even quality (scrapbook worthy versus non-scrapbook worthy). With an efficient system in place, you'll spend more time scrapbooking and less time searching.

### CREATE INVENTORY CATALOGS

Spare yourself the frustration and time wasted turning your craft room inside out to determine if you have a particular punch, stamp, sticker, paper, die and the like. Create small samplings and swatches using binders you create yourself, or fill in manufactured versions for quick and easy reference. Be sure to include details such as size, color, brand name and the like.

### SEPARATE SMALL EMBELLISHMENTS

Itty-bitty accents can cause oversized headaches when not sorted and stored properly. Avoid the annoyance of scouring your entire stash for one specific accent by stowing them inside compartmentalized containers.

# Tools

Whether you wish to enhance your page design, accents, color schemes, titles or journaling, all your bases are covered with these handy tools. Make use of these scrapbooking sidekicks and you'll minimize time and maximize results.

## COMPUTER

Technology is a beautiful thing. Make it work for you for nearly every aspect of your scrapbooking from idea inspiration to design execution. Utilize word processing programs, Internet fonts, clip art, desktop publishing programs, as well as image-editing and page layout software to easily add sophistication to your pages.

## ADHESIVE APPLICATION MACHINE

This little adhesive-application machine will fast become a much-used favorite. In an instant you can turn items like die-cut letters, fabrics and paper accents into peel-and-stick page additions.

## COLOR WHEEL

If your closest encounter with a color wheel was seeing one displayed on the wall during a high school art class, it's time you got your hands on one and got up close and personal. With a series of simple spins, you'll soon be concocting eye-catching color combinations that you otherwise wouldn't have come up with.

## DIE-CUTTING MACHINES

Die-cutting machines take the effort out of the otherwise painstaking process of handcutting page elements with precision. Alphabets, numbers, shapes, frames, tags and much more can be created in no time using interchangeable dies.

# Planning

A little foresight goes a long way when you're short on time but big on imagination. See to it that the scrapbook pages you have envisioned become a reality by contemplating your creations in advance.

## PHOTO CHECKLIST

Have an event coming up you know you want to scrapbook? You can guarantee you'll come away with all the right shots by compiling a checklist in advance. Approaching the occasion with a selective eye will make the most efficient use of your film or memory card and will make scrapbooking the resulting layouts less overwhelming. Immediately following the photo session, jot down notes to jog your memory later on.

## INSTANT MATTING

Creating artsy photographs with a formal feel is as easy as requesting bordered prints from your film developer, or by carefully trimming prints you create at home to retain a white edge. Applied directly to your page or layered with additional mats, maximum dimension will be achieved with minimal time and effort.

## PAGE KITS

Give yourself the ultimate jump-start by assembling photos, papers, embellishments and any design notes in a packet prior to sitting down to create your pages. This simple process of setting aside elements in advance will dramatically accelerate the page-creating process and will always keep you one step ahead.

## SHOPPING LISTS

Although it is enjoyable to leisurely survey each and every aisle of your favorite scrapbook store, both your schedule and your pocketbook will benefit from more focused visits. Maintain your inventory with the shopping list provided on page 13 to keep your craft supply well-stocked.

# *Designing*

It's easier than you think to put stylish and sophisticated pages together in a snap. Look for design inspiration in everyday items that could translate into page ideas. Moreover, make use of products that mimic the look of more time-intensive page additions but come page-ready.

## IDEA SKETCHBOOK

Inspiration may be gleaned from everyday sources such as newspapers and magazines, books, junk mail, brochures, postcards, menus, textiles, architecture, billboards, product packaging, nature and the like. Scribble down notes, collect swatches, cut and paste clippings and draw designs in a notebook or binder that spur your imagination for new pages.

## COORDINATING PRODUCT

Can you say "simple"? Take the guesswork out of the page-creating process with perfectly paired papers and accents guaranteed to deliver a dynamite design. No matter your theme or artistic tastes, there's sure to be a product line ideal for the layout you have envisioned.

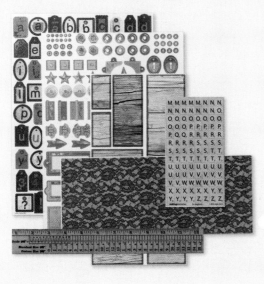

## FAUX EMBELLISHMENTS

Though faux, the dramatic impact and artistry of these page additions is very real. Instantly add the look of metal, wood, fabric and the like without adding the weight and bulk of the actual items to your page.

## PREMADE ACCENTS

Put your page over-the-top in the time it takes to break open the package. Calling upon such pre-assembled products as tags, frames, pre-stitched papers and threaded, self-adhesive buttons makes it possible to add that little something extra to your design without committing extra time.

# Journaling

No need to struggle with putting into words thoughts and emotions that are perfect for your page. Get a helpful head start with product, idea resources and quick-and-easy approaches for instant and engaging journaling.

## PREPRINTED SENTIMENTS

Couldn't have said it better yourself? Preprinted sentiments are the time-friendly solution for representing your thoughts and feelings in an artful way—all the while sparing you the pressure of waiting for your own poetic muses to descend. Never has it been so easy to express yourself with preprinted overlays, quotes and rub-ons perfect for any page.

## QUOTE BOOKS AND WEB SITES

When in search of sayings custom-suited to your subject, look to collections of quotes available in handbooks and Internet sites for a treasure trove of options. Whether you are after wisdom or whimsy, incorporating the insightful words of others adds instant insight to your layout.

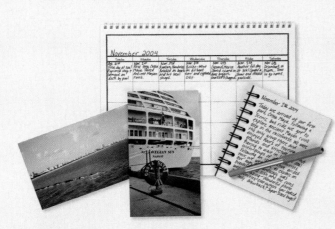

## DAILY JOURNALING

Record the whos, whats, whens, wheres and whys in a daily journal while they're fresh in your mind to save yourself hours in the long run. Keep annual calendars detailing events and occasions and attach sticky notes to the backsides of photos as soon as the prints return from the developer. In doing so you preserve precious memories and you get into the helpful habit of having the necessary details on hand for future journaling.

## OUTSIDE JOURNALING

In addition to being a fast and fun way to add journaling to a page, interviews with friends and loved ones, bits of funny dialogue with a child and other recounted conversations make it easy to include the unique perspectives of others on a page. Instead of starting from scratch, your journaling will be provided for you—simply take detailed notes, draw up a fun questionnaire or transcribe a recording.

# Speedy Shopper Checklist

Accelerate time spent shopping for supplies by determining what items need replenishing beforehand.
Photocopy this checklist for efficient shopping to avoid doubling up on or forgetting items.

## ORGANIZATIONAL SUPPLIES
- ☐ Photo box(es)
- ☐ Negative sleeves
- ☐ Photo envelopes
- ☐ Self-stick notes
- ☐ Memorabilia keepers
- ☐ Storage containers

## ALBUMS
- ☐ Strap-hinge
- ☐ Post-bound
- ☐ Spiral
- ☐ 3-Ring binder
- ☐ Mini
- ☐ Other

## ALBUM SIZES
- ☐ 6 x 6"
- ☐ 8 x 8"
- ☐ 8½ x 11"
- ☐ 12 x 12"
- ☐ 12 x 15"
- ☐ Other

## ALBUM FILLER PAGES
- ☐ 6 x 6"
- ☐ 8 x 8"
- ☐ 8½ x 11"
- ☐ 12 x 12"
- ☐ 12 x 15"
- ☐ Other

## ALBUM PAGE PROTECTORS
- ☐ 6 x 6"
- ☐ 8 x 8"
- ☐ 8½ x 11"
- ☐ 12 x 12"
- ☐ 12 x 15"
- ☐ Other

## ARCHIVAL-QUALITY ADHESIVES
- ☐ Photo splits
- ☐ Double-sided photo tape
- ☐ Tape roller
- ☐ Liquid glue pen
- ☐ Glue stick
- ☐ Self-adhesive foam spacers
- ☐ Spray adhesive
- ☐ Adhesive-application machine cartridge
- ☐ Glue dots
- ☐ Extremely tacky tape
- ☐ Adhesive remover
- ☐ Other

## SCISSORS AND CUTTERS
- ☐ Small scissors
- ☐ Regular scissors
- ☐ Paper trimmer
- ☐ Craft knife
- ☐ Punches
- ☐ Replacement blades

## PENCILS, PENS, MARKERS
- ☐ Pigment pen(s)
- ☐ Photo-safe pencil
- ☐ Colored pencils
- ☐ Vanishing ink pen
- ☐ Red eye pen
- ☐ pH testing pen

## OTHER COLORANTS
- ☐ Dye ink
- ☐ Pigment ink
- ☐ Embossing ink
- ☐ Solvent ink
- ☐ Distress ink
- ☐ Chalk ink
- ☐ Metallic ink
- ☐ Watermark ink
- ☐ Acrylic paint
- ☐ Pigment paint
- ☐ Pigment powder
- ☐ Metallic rub-ons
- ☐ Chalk
- ☐ Stamp cleaner

*Types and colors*

## RULERS AND TEMPLATES
- ☐ Metal straightedge ruler
- ☐ Grid ruler
- ☐ Shape template(s)
- ☐ Letter template(s)
- ☐ Nested template(s)

## ACID- AND LIGNIN-FREE PAPER
- ☐ Cardstock
- ☐ Patterned paper
- ☐ Vellum
- ☐ Specialty paper
- ☐ Other

*Types and Colors*

## STICKERS
- ☐ Themed
- ☐ 3-Dimensional
- ☐ Alphabet
- ☐ Other

## DIE CUTS
*Themes or types*

## RUBBER STAMPS
- ☐ Themed
- ☐ Textured background
- ☐ Alphabet

## EMBELLISHMENTS
- ☐ Metal
- ☐ Acrylic
- ☐ Ribbon
- ☐ Fibers
- ☐ Tags
- ☐ Organics
- ☐ Eyelets and brads
- ☐ Beads
- ☐ Buttons
- ☐ Other

# CHAPTER ONE
## *sketches*

BEST FRIENDS

Dewey and Daniel seem to have such a special relationship, sometimes they are buddies, sometimes they are rivals for Daddy's attention, and sometimes they just simply like to hang out. It is not unusual to hear complaining from Daniel when Dewey snatches his toys and it is also not unusual to see Dewey acting restless when Daniel is playing with Dewey's toys. Neither one likes to share, unless it is dinner time and Daniel isn't hungry, as we can usually find Dewey under the table waiting for Daniel to feed him dinner. Trouble A and Trouble B is what they are affectionately known as, but we would have it no other way, as it makes Mommy and Daddy happy to see such a happy pair.

## Two Peas in a Bucket

### BREAK A PAGE INTO THIRDS

An enlarged and vertically cropped photo provided dual meaning for both Jessie's children and her favorite Internet scrapbooking site. Print title vertically on green textured cardstock background. Print journaling on blue textured cardstock; cut out and mount. Cut strip of dark blue cardstock; ink edges in black and mount across bottom of page. Crop and mount enlarged photo. Cut square from green textured cardstock, ink edges and adhere. Add stitching detail to two metal tin accents and apply stamps to smaller tin with solvent ink; mount with foam adhesive. Handwrite journaling on bottom left corner to complete.

*Jessie Baldwin, Las Vegas, Nevada*

**SUPPLIES:** Green and light blue textured cardstock (Bazzill); stitched tin tiles (Making Memories); letter stamps (Hero Arts); black solvent ink (Tsukineko); dark blue cardstock; fibers for stitching; foam adhesive; black pen

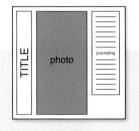

## Family 04

### ENVELOP A PAGE WITH AN ENLARGEMENT

Leah made excellent use of her page space with an enlarged, embellished photo. Print journaling onto bottom of red cardstock background; mount photo above, adding strip of textured pink cardstock along bottom. Layer decorative clip onto photo with textured cardstock and attach metal tag with brads. Stamp title onto patterned paper square; add brad. Apply date with stamp and layered metal number charms. Finish page by adhering tied ribbon.

*Leah LaMontagne, Las Vegas, Nevada*

**SUPPLIES:** Pink textured cardstock (Bazzill); decorative clip (Scrapworks); metal tag (Jo-Ann Fabric); patterned paper (Karen Foster Design); letter stamps (Stampabilities); date stamp, metal number 4 charm (Making Memories); punched number, metal charm (Colorbök); red cardstock; brads

## Lillian

### DIVIDE PAGE SPACE INTO QUADRANTS

Sara-Jane created a bold and graphic page with quadrants and an understated title placement. Print title and journaling on bottom left corner of white cardstock background. Cut section of garden patterned paper and sections and strips of black, red and yellow cardstocks; layer all onto background page with photo. Paint decorative brad yellow. Attach silk flower with painted brad.

*Sara-Jane Bunting, Orakei, Auckland, New Zealand*

**SUPPLIES:** Patterned paper (Rusty Pickle); decorative brad (Making Memories); white, black, red and yellow cardstocks; silk flower; yellow paint

It is so nice that Max has a friend who is a girl and just as well that he has chosen you as your parents are such good friends of ours. Even though you are two years older you actually have a lot in common. I hope you will help me teach him about females and the way we think so that when he is older he is still a kind sensitive guy. I'm glad you are around

Lillian

ROUT'S SEED HOUSE
PORTAGE LA PRAIRIE, MANITOBA
CARNATION

BRETT-YOUNG SEEDS LTD.
410 CORYDON AVE., WINNIPEG
ZINNIA
DWARF LILLIPUT

PROUT

HIB

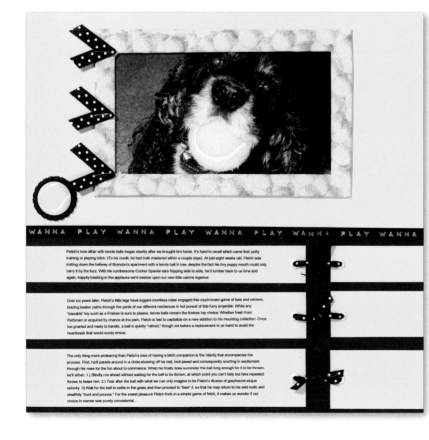

## Wanna Play

### JOURNAL ON STRIPS

Emily maximized her single-page space with an oversized slide mount frame and strip-style journaling. Cover top half of black cardstock background with yellow cardstock. Journal on yellow cardstock; cut into sections and mount across bottom of page. Tie sections together with polka-dot ribbon threaded through eyelets set at the end of each strip. Create label title; affix across center of page. Cut oversized slide mount with craft knife to accommodate photo. Adhere photo to page. Wrap slide mount with sanded ball-patterned paper; adhere over photo. Adorn with stapled black polka-dot ribbon. Paint bottle cap with black acrylic paint and mount on page, affixing ball sticker inside.

*Emily Curry Hitchingham, Memory Makers Books*

**SUPPLIES:** Label (Dymo); oversized slide mount (Jest Charming); patterned paper (Frances Meyer); bottle cap, ball sticker (Design Originals); black and yellow cardstocks; eyelets; black polka-dot ribbon; craft knife; sandpaper; stapler; black acrylic paint

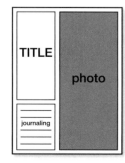

Daniel and Angel, sometimes, ok, a lot of the time you fight like cats and dogs, but there are moments like this one that take my breath away. I love when the two of you play together and act like you are truly friends like I hope you will always be. My wish for the two of you is that you always lean on each other for love and support, after all you both must always remember that when you get older there is no other friend in the world like your sibling.

March 2004

## *I Love My 2 Sweet Babies*
### DESIGN FROM SIDE TO SIDE

Michelle's title, photo and journaling all artfully parallel each other and span the entire width of the page. Enlarge photo and mount on black textured cardstock background with black photo corners. Cut various patterned paper strips; ink edges in black and layer along top and bottom of page. Machine stitch edges of smaller strips. Form title using letter stickers and punch-out word covered with concho. Accent with hearts cut from black textured cardstock. Journal on transparency; cut out and adhere along bottom of page.

*Michelle Tornay, Newark, California*

**SUPPLIES:** Black textured cardstock (Bazzill); black photo corners (Canson); patterned paper (Chatterbox); letter stickers (Me & My Big Ideas); punch-out word (KI Memories); concho (Scrapworks); black ink

## *...Growing Up*
### CREATE A BOLD TITLE BLOCK

Katherine reinforced her enlarged vertical photo with a bold title treatment. Begin by printing blue title block and journaling on white cardstock background; leave space in title block for square paper embellishment. Cut section of striped patterned paper and mount vertically on right side of page; crop enlarged photo and adhere vertically over striped section. Mat punch-out word on polka-dot patterned paper; adhere on title block.

*Katherine Teague, New Westminster, British Columbia, Canada*

**SUPPLIES:** Striped and polka-dot patterned papers, punch-out word (KI Memories); white cardstock

Mackenzie, as I looked at this photo of you playing at the park, I realized that you are growing up. That day at the park was the first day that you swung in the swings happily and without fear. You also climbed right onto the teeter-totter and proceeded to rock back and forth with vigour. Right before our eyes, you are becoming a little girl A girl who can go to the park and play and interact with all of the playground equipment rather than a baby who admired the fun from afar. Rock away my little Mack.

## The Horse Whisperer

### PUNCH UP A SINGLE PHOTO PAGE

Jodi created an attractive sense of balance on her single photo page with an assortment of punched squares. Sand, crumple and flatten rust-colored patterned paper and mount on black cardstock. Punch, crumple, sand and flatten squares from various patterned papers. Arrange along one side of page, adding threaded self-adhesive buttons. Print journaling onto patterned paper, cut out and mount. Add enlarged photo printed with title. Cut cowgirl element from patterned paper and add to bottom of page.

*Jodi Amidei, Memory Makers Books*

**SUPPLIES:** Patterned papers (Deluxe Designs, Flair Designs, Paper Adventures, Scenic Route Paper Co.); buttons (EK Success); black cardstock

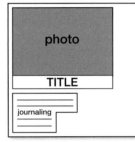

## Jordan

### GO VERTICAL WITH A TITLE

A vertical title artfully offsets a single photo and journaling block. Tear large section of patterned paper; mount on pink cardstock background. Add die-cut letter title down right side. Set three pairs of eyelets at approximately 4" intervals along paper seams. Thread ribbon through eyelets in crisscross fashion, securing ends on back of page. Mount photo printed with white border on patterned paper using foam adhesive; accent with word charms. Mount vellum journaling block with eyelets; thread with ribbon and tie. Cut dolls from patterned paper; mount. Wrap one page corner with ribbon. Add detail throughout page with glitter glue.

*Jodi Amidei, Memory Makers Books*

**SUPPLIES:** Patterned papers (Rusty Pickle) word charms (Making Memories) die-cut letters (QuicKutz); glitter glue (Ranger); ribbon (Offray); pink eyelets

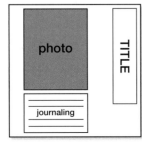

## Top Three Things That I Love About You
### SECTION-OFF PAGE SPACE

This graphic page draws the eye with a vertical title and bold sections. Anne created her layout using Paint Shop Pro software, but you can easily re-create it in traditional fashion. First print journaling on textured light blue cardstock, trimming one side to layer over an 8½ x 11" textured blue cardstock background. Layer with an enlarged black-and-white photo mounted on an oversized white cardstock mat. Add circles punched from textured yellow, orange and light blue cardstocks. Create portion of title with stamps, and mount die cut word to bottom of photo. Add thin black cardstock strips to top and bottom of white cardstock section. Embellish journaling block with stamped tag applied with brads.

*Anne Langpap, La Verne, California*

**SUPPLIES:** Textured light blue, blue, yellow and orange cardstocks; rubber stamps; white and black cardstocks; white tag; black brads; circle punch; die-cut word Digital image-editing software: Paint Shop Pro (Corel)

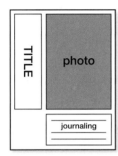

THINGS THAT I LOVE ABOUT YOU...

*three*

1) You're always so happy to see me when we've been apart. Even if I walk outside to take out the trash, you greet me with such love when I return. 2) You give the best hugs! You wrap your arms around my neck and won't let go. I love it! 3) You make me laugh every day. Whether you're making funny faces or copying Taylor's ballet dancing, you keep me smiling!

• JUNE 2004 •

bundLed up

## Bundled Up
### COMPOSE A GRAPHIC LAYOUT

Danielle was influenced to do this single-photo layout by an advertisement she saw in a magazine. Print title and poem on bottom right corner of patterned paper background. Adhere enlarged photo to page. Apply title to photo with rub-on words.

*Danielle Christian, Cumming, Georgia*

**SUPPLIES:** Patterned paper, circle tag (KI Memories); rub-on words (Making Memories)

## Sibling Unity

### SUPPLEMENT A SINGLE LARGE PHOTO

Amy captured the essence of her friend's children as well as their individual personalities in an enlarged black-and-white group photo supplemented with individual color photos. Ink brown textured cardstock background with dark brown; adhere inked patterned paper strips on top and bottom. Journal on white cardstock; ink edges and adhere. Lightly edge photos in dark brown ink and layer onto page with preprinted twill stickers on top and bottom of photos. Adorn page with brads and acrylic bauble; handwrite date. Staple letter stencil backed with patterned paper onto top of photo; handwrite name.

*Amy Howe, Frisco, Texas*
*Photos and journaling: Felicia Krelwitz, Lake Zurich, Illinois*

**SUPPLIES:** Brown textured cardstock (Bazzill); striped and blue patterned paper, acrylic bauble (KI Memories); preprinted twill stickers (Pebbles); dark brown ink; white cardstock; brads; letter stencil; staple; pen

## Pure Baby

### FRAME CROPPED PHOTOS

Jlyne created an eye-catching assemblage of cropped photos and papers in the center of her layout. Crop photos and various patterned papers; ink edges of papers with distress ink. Mount together on center of a denim textured cardstock background; affix letter sticker on bottom right patterned paper section. Apply rub-on words on patterned paper strips. Tie various ribbons onto molding strip and attach diagonally across bottom of page with square brads. Journal around photos with black pen.

*Jlyne Hanback, Biloxi, Mississippi*

**SUPPLIES:** Patterned papers, denim textured cardstock, letter sticker, rub-on words; molding strip (Chatterbox); tea stained distress ink (Ranger); various ribbons; square brads; pen

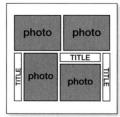

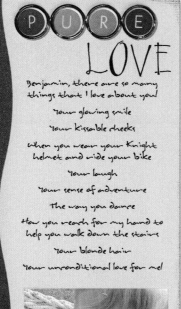

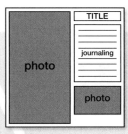

## Pure Love
### EDGE AN ENLARGED PHOTO

Shandy cut her cropped and enlarged photo with a wavy edge for visual interest. Ink edges of green textured cardstock background with green ink; journal on right side of page. Enlarge photo and cut right edge in a slight wave; mount on left side of page. Cut strip of red textured cardstock in same pattern and mount over photo edge. Cut section of drywall tape; ink in green and layer with smaller photo. For title, affix letter stickers on page and frame with key rings. Apply rub-on letters for remainder of title.

*Shandy Vogt, Nampa, Idaho*

**SUPPLIES:** Green and red textured cardstocks (Bazzill); letter stickers (EK Success); rub-on letters (Making Memories); green ink; drywall tape; key rings

## Taking a Hike
### OFFSET A LARGE PHOTO

Stacy used two cropped photos in one page corner to offset her enlarged focal shot. Begin by layering various cut patterned papers onto blue textured cardstock background; print journaling on one section and stamp title onto others. Affix rickrack at edges of patterned papers. Using a dry brush, lightly edge photos with cream acrylic paint; mount on page. Mat punch-out words onto textured cardstock then onto metal-rimmed tags; lightly brush rims with paint and mount.

*Stacy Yoder, Yucaipa, California*

**SUPPLIES:** Blue textured cardstock (Bazzill); patterned papers, punch-out words (KI Memories); letter stamps (Ma Vinci's Reliquary, PSX Design); rickrack; paintbrush; cream acrylic paint; metal-rimmed tags

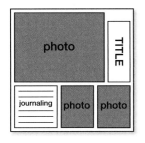

## Flying High...
### STACK SEQUENTIAL PHOTOS

Kathleen used two stacked photos on a single, simple page that shows the joy of her son taking "flight" in his father's outstretched hands. Mount photos on right side of olive cardstock background. Print title and journaling on light green cardstock; cut out, mat on dark green cardstock and adhere on left side of page.

*Kathleen Payne, Norfolk, Virginia*

**SUPPLIES:** Olive, dark green and cream cardstocks

### FLYING HIGH
with Daddy

Look at you, my SWEET BABY CHARLES. You are so content and giggly, FLYING HIGH in the sky on DADDY'S STRONG HANDS. I love witnessing this POWERFUL MOMENT in time. Daddy is giving you, our seven-month-old son, an AIRPLANE RIDE.

Do you already instinctively know that DADDY IS STRONG so that you, as an infant, don't have to be?

Or is that happiness spread across your face because you know DADDY IS STRONG ENOUGH to ever so gently hold you in his arms?

My heart bursts with pride as I listen to Daddy tell you, "I LOVE YOU BABY CHARLIE, I LOVE YOU, I LOVE YOU, I LOVE YOU."

Keep smiling my son. Enjoy the LASTING SECURITY of DADDY'S LOVING HANDS.

Your airplane ride from Daddy may be short lived, but HE WILL NEVER LET YOU DOWN. This I know.

## A Cluster of Cousins
### ALIGN SEVERAL CROPPED PHOTOS

Belinda was inspired to do this layout by a menu at McDonald's that featured individual photos of their desserts. Print title and date on bottom of green textured cardstock background. Cut section of light green textured cardstock and print information that coordinates with photos to be mounted; mount photos. Stitch piece onto background over red cardstock strips; enhance edges with metallic rub-ons. Stitch heart torn from red cardstock and enhanced with metallic rub-ons and chalk onto bottom of page with floss. Adorn opposite bottom corner with sewn buttons.

*Belinda Buchanan, Narrandera, Australia*

**SUPPLIES:** Green textured cardstocks (Bazzill); metallic rub-ons, chalk (Craf-T); red cardstock; floss; buttons

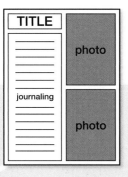

## Sam

### SHOWCASE SEQUENTIAL PHOTOS

Beth used a series of expressive photos to offer a glimpse into her son's personality. Adhere same-sized photos across the center of a blue textured cardstock background. Print title and subtitles onto green textured cardstock; cut and mount along with patterned paper strips on bottom of page.

*Beth Proudfoot, Clinton, New Jersey*

**SUPPLIES:** Blue and green textured cardstocks (Bazzill); patterned paper (Chatterbox)

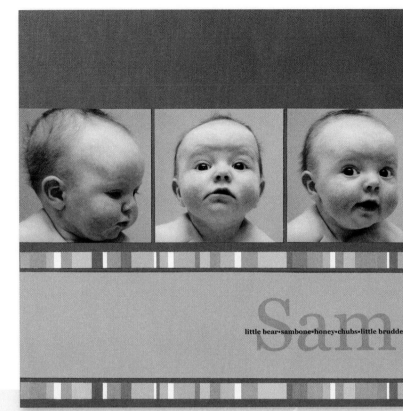

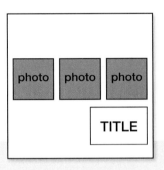

## Popsicle

### ARTFULLY ARRANGE PHOTOS

Rebecca created a graphic layout using a series of photos featuring her daughter's new favorite pastime. Print title on top and journaling on bottom of white cardstock background. Crop photos and mount in a grouping on page. Cut a strip of green striped patterned paper and strip of blue polka-dot patterned paper; mount on page above and below photos.

*Rebecca Cooper, Raymond, Alberta, Canada*

**SUPPLIES:** Green striped and blue polka-dot patterned papers (Beary Patch); white cardstock

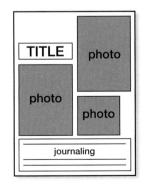

## Remember This
### FEATURE PHOTOS WITH SIMPLICITY

Beth created a timeless layout showcasing her photos by keeping them the focus as opposed to a lot of embellishments. Begin by printing journaling and title on purple textured cardstock background. Mount photo onto page, affixing black mat atop it. Adhere strip of lighter purple textured cardstock on bottom of page and adorn with cropped photos. Print date in white onto black cardstock; cut to fit beneath metal-rimmed tag, attach with eyelet and tie off with ribbon.

*Beth Proudfoot, Clinton, New Jersey*
*Photos: Timothy A. Murphy Photography, Richmond, Virginia*

**SUPPLIES:** Purple textured cardstocks (Bazzill); black mat; white cardstock; metal-rimmed tag and ribbon (Making Memories); eyelet

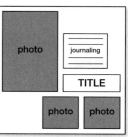

## Smile
### CLUSTER PHOTOS IN ONE CORNER

Dawn celebrated a special personality with photos assembled to one side of her page. Adhere white mesh across lower part of patterned paper background. Mat photos on backside of same patterned paper; bend upper right corner on focal photo over and attach swirl clip. Slip date printed on torn purple vellum piece under clip and adhere photos on page. Journal on clear vellum; mount. Apply title on page with die-cut letters. Embellish patterned paper tag with sections of white mesh, torn vellum, patterned paper and small envelope. Slip smaller tag adorned with letter stickers and eyelet inside envelope, adding pressed flowers. Tie off with fibers and mount on page.

*Dawn Burden, Franklin, Tennessee*

**SUPPLIES:** White mesh (Magic Mesh); patterned paper background (Color-bök); swirl clip (Making Memories); die-cut letters (My Mind's Eye); envelope template (Hot Off The Press); letter stickers (Creative Imaginations); pressed flowers (Pressed Petals); purple and clear vellum; eyelet; fibers

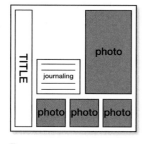

## Time Flies

### SHOWCASE CONTRASTING PHOTOS

Amanda photographed both the serious and playful sides of her sister and coordinated the layout in black and gray. Journal onto gray cardstock; trim and mat piece onto black cardstock background. Adhere strip of patterned paper vertically off center on background. Mount photos and punch-outs; add handwritten date to finish.

*Amanda Goodwin, Munroe Falls, Ohio*

**SUPPLIES:** Patterned paper, punch-outs (KI Memories); gray and black cardstocks; pen

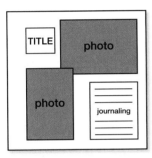

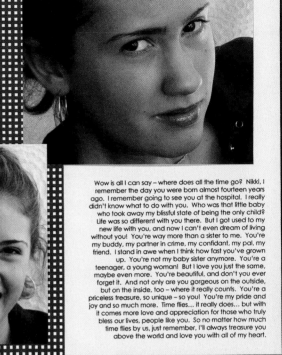

Wow is all I can say – where does all the time go? Nikki, I remember the day you were born almost fourteen years ago. I remember going to see you at the hospital. I really didn't know what to do with you. Who was that little baby who took away my blissful state of being the only child? Life was so different with you there. But I got used to my new life with you, and now I can't even dream of living without you! You're way more than a sister to me. You're my buddy, my partner in crime, my confidant, my pal, my friend. I stand in awe when I think how fast you've grown up. You're not my baby sister anymore. You're a teenager, a young woman! But I love you just the same, maybe even more. You're beautiful, and don't you ever forget it. And not only are you gorgeous on the outside, but on the inside, too – where it really counts. You're a priceless treasure, so unique – so you! You're my pride and joy and so much more. Time flies... it really does... but with it comes more love and appreciation for those who truly bless our lives, people like you. So no matter how much time flies by us, just remember, I'll always treasure you above the world and love you with all of my heart.

## Art Is Man's Nature...

### BREAK A PAGE INTO BLOCKS

Maria created a striking, geometric look in her design to complement the granite sculpture in her photos. Apply metallic rub-ons onto white cardstock; trim and mat piece onto green cardstock background. Uniformly crop photos and pieces of green cardstock into squares, matting desired photos; mount all onto page. Adhere die-cut letters on green squares and handwrite date to complete.

*Maria Williams, Cary, North Carolina*

**SUPPLIES:** Paper (Club Scrap); metallic rub-ons (Jacquard Products); die-cut letters (QuickKutz); white and green cardstocks; pen

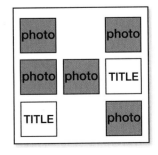

## Reflections of 2003
### PARALLEL PAGE ELEMENTS

Valerie created a well-balanced layout by mirroring her cropped photo border with her title bar and also in the arrangement of her focal photos. Begin by printing words in various fonts on center of light blue cardstock background; mount with larger photos. Print title on piece of light blue cardstock; cut and mat on white cardstock and adhere on top of page. Adorn title with metal photo corners. Punch remaining photos with square punch and affix along bottom of page. Adhere rickrack to finish.

*Valerie Barton, Flowood, Mississippi*

**SUPPLIES:** Metal photo corners (Making Memories); square punch (McGill); light blue and white cardstocks; rickrack

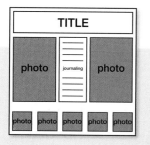

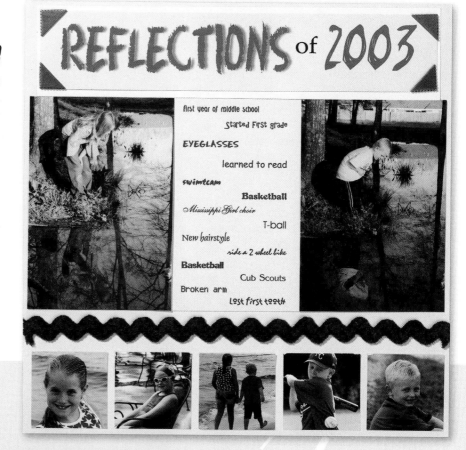

## The Puyallup Fair
### CONSERVE SPACE WITH CLUSTERED PHOTOS

Angela concentrated photos in one area of her page to free up more room for journaling. Journal onto white textured cardstock background; adhere pictures side by side. Affix ribbon along right edge of photos. Mount section of blue cardstock horizontally along bottom of page along with ribbon; apply title with letter stickers. Mix shades of blue acrylic paint with white and apply to metal photo corner; once dry, mount on upper left corner to complete.

*Angela Marvel, Puyallup, Washington*

**SUPPLIES:** White textured cardstock background (Bazzill); letter stickers (Creative Imaginations); metal photo corner (Making Memories); ribbon; blue cardstock; various blue and white acrylic paints

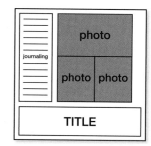

## My Snowman
### SPLIT PAGE SPACE WITH A BAR

Nancy used a stamped bar featuring cropped photos to help showcase her son's frolic in the snow. Cut section from white cardstock for bottom border. Stamp with snowflake and various square images using blue and gray inks; wrap with ribbon. Mat section on dark blue cardstock; tear edges and mount on bottom of light blue cardstock background. Mat focal photo and square-punched photos on dark blue cardstock and mount. Journal on white cardstock; cut out and mat on dark blue cardstock. Add title with letter stamps and strip cut from dark blue cardstock; handwrite date in blue below. Mount piece on page.

*Nancy Kliewer, Fairfax, Virginia*

**SUPPLIES:** Various snowflake and square stamps, letter stamps (Stampin' Up!); white, dark blue, and light blue cardstocks; ribbon; small square punch; blue pen

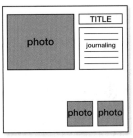

## First Crush
### DISPLAY A PHOTO SEQUENCE

Cherie used a series of photos to show the many faces of her darling little boy. Ink edges of purple textured cardstock background with black ink; cut sections of striped patterned paper, ink edges and mount throughout page. Accent smaller photos with black photo corners; adhere to page. Double mat focal photo on white and purple textured cardstocks, inking edges in black; add photo corners. Cut larger mat from green textured cardstock, round corners, ink edges and affix on page; add striped patterned paper strip and double-matted photo. Journal on cream-colored textured cardstock; cut out, leaving room for title block and folded ribbons attached with staples. Ink edges in purple and adhere. Stamp title onto blue textured cardstock; cut out and mount over journal block. Apply rub-on date to brown cardstock; trim and mount beneath label holder. Suspend with gingham ribbon and embellish with bottle cap and button.

*Cherie A. Ward, Colorado Springs, Colorado*

**SUPPLIES:** Purple, white, green, and blue textured cardstocks (Bazzill); striped patterned paper (KI Memories); black photo corners (Pioneer); letter stamps (Ma Vinci's Reliquary); rub-on date (Autumn Leaves); label holder (Making Memories); bottle cap (Li'l Davis Designs); button (Doodlebug Design); black and purple inks; various ribbons; staples; brown cardstock

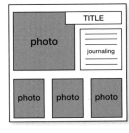

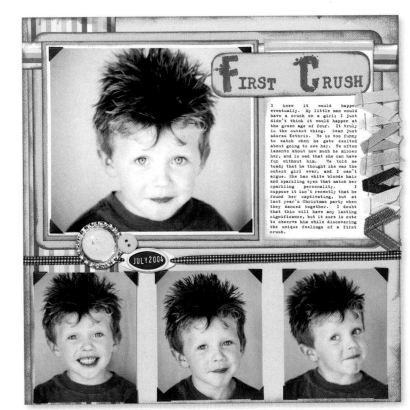

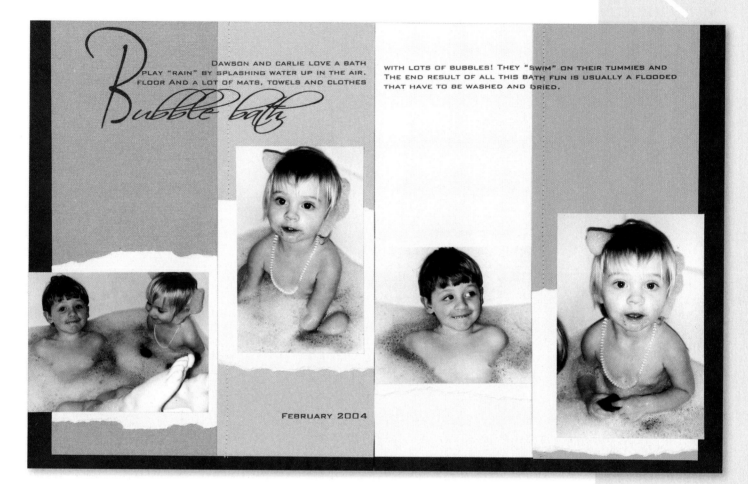

DAWSON AND CARLIE LOVE A BATH
PLAY "RAIN" BY SPLASHING WATER UP IN THE AIR.
FLOOR AND A LOT OF MATS, TOWELS AND CLOTHES

WITH LOTS OF BUBBLES! THEY "SWIM" ON THEIR TUMMIES AND
THE END RESULT OF ALL THIS BATH FUN IS USUALLY A FLOODED
THAT HAVE TO BE WASHED AND DRIED.

*Bubble bath*

FEBRUARY 2004

## Bubble Bath

### DISPLAY PHOTOS AND JOURNALING ON STRIPS

These bold and vibrantly colored cardstock strips comprise an appealing way to showcase photos across a two-page spread. Start with two black cardstock backgrounds. Cut vertical sections of textured pink, orange, yellow and green cardstocks and layer in pairs onto each page; machine stitch where strips overlap. Print journaling onto tops of both pages; print date on bottom of left page and title on top of left page. Create mats for photos from white textured cardstock in the width of the cardstock strips; tear top and bottom edges, mount with photos and adhere to each section.

*Dana Swords, Doswell, Virginia*

**SUPPLIES:** Pink, orange, yellow, green and white textured cardstocks (Bazzill); black cardstock

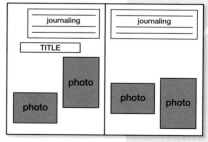

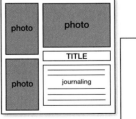

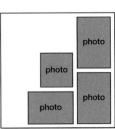

# Christmas at Our House

### PLAY WITH SPACE IN YOUR PAGE DESIGN

Brandi designed a spread about her love of decorating for Christmas using clusters of photos along the periphery of her page, creating artistic areas of "white space." Begin with two light green textured cardstock backgrounds. Cut and adhere sections of rust-colored patterned paper for page borders. Journal onto darker green textured cardstock, leaving room for focal photo. Adhere focal photo along with title tag, tying each end with gingham ribbon. Wrap around journaling box and adhere on left page. Mount all remaining photos.

*Brandi Barnes, Kelso, Tennessee*

**SUPPLIES:** Light green and darker green textured cardstocks (Bazzill); rust-colored patterned paper, punch-out title tag (Chatterbox); gingham ribbon (Offray)

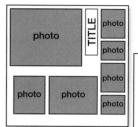

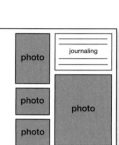

## Tess & Cody
### MAXIMIZE YOUR PAGE SPACE

Heather employed strategic cropping and placement to accommodate many photos on two
pages. For the left page, cut and layer striped and
polka-dot patterned papers and dark pink paper
onto light pink background. Mat focal photo on
white cardstock; ink edges in brown and mount
on upper left corner of page. Crop and adhere
remaining photos. Apply title with letter stickers;
handwrite date in black pen. For right page, cut
and layer striped and polka-dot patterned papers,
light pink and taupe papers onto a dark pink
background. Adhere focal photo on bottom right
corner of page; crop and mount remaining photos. Journal on upper right corner of page; add
pink brad. Affix ribbon across bottom of page.

*Heather Awsumb, Silver Spring, Maryland*

**SUPPLIES:** Striped and polka-dot patterned papers (KI Memories); letter
stickers (Me & My Big Ideas); ribbon (Making Memories); light pink, dark
pink and taupe papers; white cardstock; brown ink; pen; pink brad

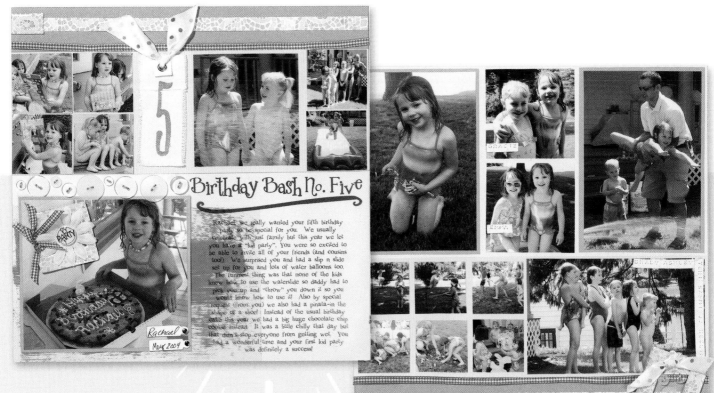

## Birthday Bash #5

### CROP PHOTOS TO FILL SPACE

Jennifer made the most of a two-page spread with strategically cropped and placed photos. Begin with two white textured cardstock backgrounds. Adhere thin strips of patterned paper on two strips of pink textured cardstock; mount on top of left page and bottom of right page, adorning with pink gingham ribbon. On left page, cluster cropped photos onto green textured cardstock mat, leaving room for canvas tag; mount. Stamp number onto canvas tag in pink ink; tie off with polka-dot ribbon and adhere on photo mat. Cut two sections of transparency; use pink acrylic paint on one section and print title and journaling on the other. Layer both with focal photo matted on light blue textured cardstock. Adhere acrylic bauble and slide mount on patterned paper; cut out and mount on page, adding gingham ribbons, party sticker and paper flower on slide mount. Handwrite on mini tags; ink edges and attach on photo with silver brads. Adorn page with clear and opaque buttons stitched on with pink floss. Repeat process for right page, adding inked labels onto corresponding photos.

*Jennifer Cupp, Rock Island, Illinois*

**SUPPLIES:** White, pink, green and light blue textured cardstocks (Bazzill, National Cardstock); patterned paper (Frances Meyer); number stamp (Making Memories); acrylic bauble, canvas tag, party sticker and slide mounts (Creative Imaginations); label maker (Dymo); pink gingham ribbon; pink ink; pink acrylic paint; polka-dot ribbon; transparency; paper flower; mini tags; silver brads; clear and opaque buttons; pink floss

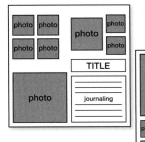

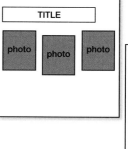

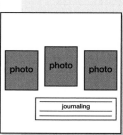

## Blue-Eyed Boy

### SPAN A SEQUENCE ACROSS TWO PAGES

For a striking look, a series of photos span a two-page spread with a continuous mat. Begin with two dark blue cardstock backgrounds. Cut two sections of light blue cardstock for photo mats; mount mats across center of pages. Adhere cropped photos in staggered fashion onto mats. Apply photo captions above and below photos with letter stickers. Cut two strips of red cardstock and two rectangles of white cardstock; mount strips across bottoms of pages, adding white rectangles. Apply title and name with letter stickers on left page. Journal onto transparency; cut out and mount over red cardstock strip on right page.

*Lynda Sturney, Calgary, Alberta, Canada*

**SUPPLIES:** Small and large letter stickers (SEI); dark blue, light blue, red and white cardstocks; transparency

## The Sweetest Thing
### CROP PHOTOS IN SEVERAL SIZES

Shannon crafted a fun spread showing off various-sized photos from a fun afternoon of picture-taking with her son. Begin with two red cardstock backgrounds. Trim sections of patterned paper for top and bottom of both pages; adhere onto both. Cut two thin strips of red cardstock and mount on bottom of both pages. Mount all photos. Apply title on left page with letter stickers and date on right page with number stickers. Journal on upper right corner of right page and embellish with zipper pulls to finish.

*Shannon Taylor, Bristol, Tennessee*

**SUPPLIES:** Patterned paper (Close To My Heart); letter and number stickers (Making Memories); zipper pulls (Junkitz); red cardstock

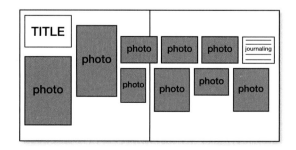

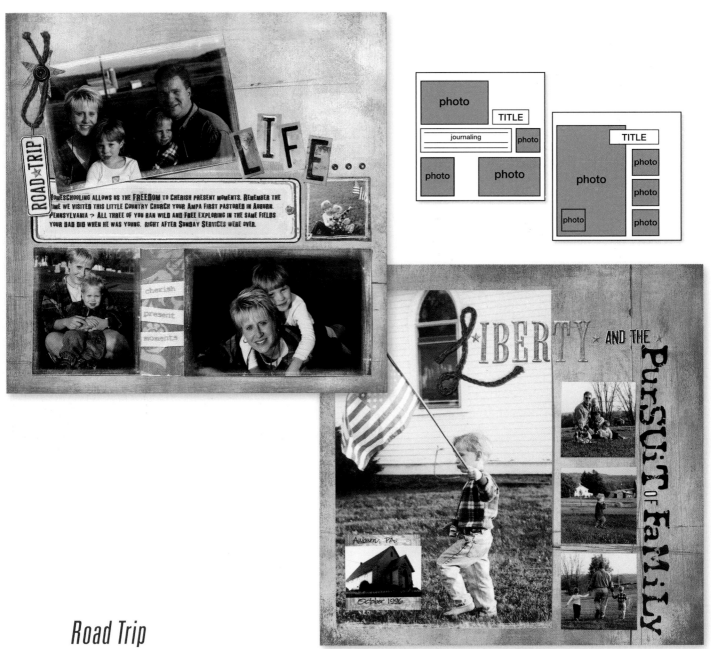

## *Road Trip*
### COMBINE ENLARGED AND CROPPED PHOTOS

Deb strategically utilized her page space through enlarging, cropping and creative placement to showcase several photos. Begin with two faux-paint patterned paper backgrounds. For left page, crop photos and sand edges. Add license plate sticker featuring journaling printed on self-adhesive vellum. Mount two photos onto patterned paper accented with printed twill. Affix remaining photos alongside tag accent. Accent top photo with fiber and decorative brad applied to star sticker. Staple smaller license plate sticker onto fiber. Apply portion of title with letter stickers; set three eyelets for ellipses. For right page, sand bottom of enlarged photo; mount along with small photo layered over patterned paper element. Crop remaining photos and adhere. Add title with various letter stickers and self-adhesive stitched letter. Accent with star stickers.

*Deb Perry, Newport News, Virginia*

**SUPPLIES:** Patterned papers (Basic Grey); license plate stickers (Paper Loft); decorative brad (Making Memories); star stickers (Mrs. Grossman's); various letter stickers (Creative Imaginations, Paper Loft, Sticker Studio); self-adhesive stitched letter (Colorbök); sandpaper; blank twill tape; self-adhesive vellum; fibers; eyelets; black pen

## Winter in Chicago
### CROP AND STACK SEVERAL SHOTS

Jane created a wintry scene on her two-page spread that showcases stacked and grouped photos. Begin with two white cardstock backgrounds. Cut sections, circles and half circles from red, black and white cardstocks and blocks from patterned paper; ink edges in black and white inks as desired. Mount cardstock sections on pages; layer photos, half circles, circles, snowman punch-outs and patterned paper blocks over both. Create title with letter stickers and stamps for left page. Journal on large circle in upper right corner on right page, stamping words in desired areas. Stamp date on bottom of journaling circle. Apply rub-on words throughout spread to complete.

*Jane Hasty, Chicago, Illinois*

**SUPPLIES:** Patterned paper, snowman punch-outs (Frances Meyer); letter stickers (Me & My Big Ideas); letter stamps (PSX Design); rub-on words (Making Memories); date stamp (source unknown); red, black and white cardstocks; white and black inks

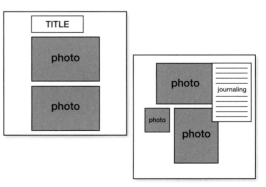

# CHAPTER TWO
## *backgrounds*

## Come Out And Play
### COLOR BLOCK A BACKGROUND

JoAnne created a background to play off of the hues in her son's outfit. Cut two sections from blue textured cardstock and mount on a blue speckled cardstock background. Affix gingham ribbon along paper seams. Mat photo on blue textured cardstock and adhere. Stamp name under photo and date on bottom left corner with letter and number stamps. Apply rub-on words on blue textured cardstock sections. Cut square piece from blue textured cardstock and adhere to metal-rimmed tag; set eyelet in corner. Apply rub-on sun; tie off with fiber and mount on intersection of gingham ribbons.

*JoAnne Bacon, Alpharetta, Georgia*

**SUPPLIES:** Blue textured and blue speckled cardstocks (Bazzill); letter and number stamps (Hero Arts); rub-on words, rub-on sun, metal-rimmed tag (Making Memories); gingham ribbons

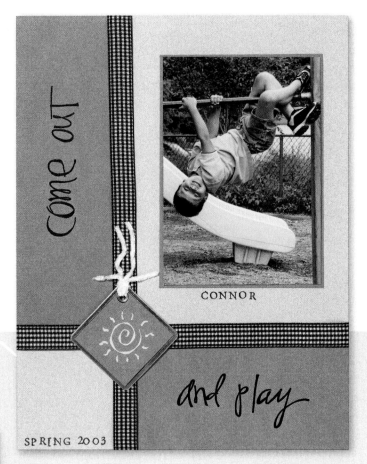

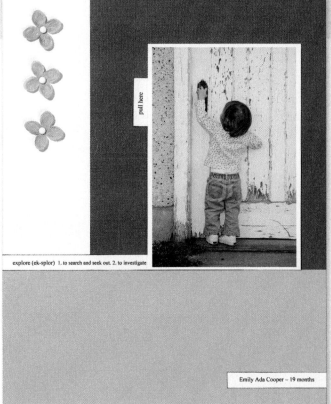

## Exploring
### COLOR BLOCK A SIMPLE BACKGROUND

Rebecca created a simple background to showcase her black-and-white photo. Begin with a textured cream-colored cardstock background. Cut sections of green and brown textured cardstocks; adhere on background page. Print title, definition, name and age on cream textured cardstock; cut into strips, ink edges in black and mount. Adhere photo, leaving center un-adhered to accommodate journaling tag. Journal on textured cream cardstock; cut into block and accent with cut and inked pull tab. Slide block behind photo. Embellish page with silk flowers attached with brads.

*Rebecca Cooper, Raymond, Alberta, Canada*

**SUPPLIES:** Textured cream, green and brown cardstocks (Bazzill)); silk flowers (Wal-Mart); black ink; brads

pull here

We've always called you 'busy.' The little girl who's always into everything! But maybe a better word for you would just be curious! You're always looking for something to get into, a new place to explore & new things to try! Our busy little, curious little girl!

## The Pout
### COLOR BLOCK WITH PATTERNED PAPERS

Cheery patterned papers were color blocked to form a background to offset the mood of Cari's daughter in the photo. Cut sections of various patterned papers; mount on orange textured cardstock background. Mat photo on black cardstock. Journal on green textured cardstock and cut out, leaving room to adhere matted photo; mount. Using computer font as guide, cut out large letter from black cardstock and portion of title from green textured cardstock; ink green edges. Double mat large letter on patterned paper and black cardstock; adhere. Mount with label sticker on bottom of page. Finish with knotted gingham ribbon affixed across paper seams.

*Cari Locken, Edmonton, Alberta, Canada*

**SUPPLIES:** Various patterned papers (Chatterbox, 7 Gypsies); orange and green textured cardstocks (Bazzill); label sticker (Pebbles); black ink; gingham ribbon

## Simple Delights
### COLOR BLOCK WITH SOLIDS AND PATTERNS

Here color-blocked patterned papers provide a perfect backdrop for a black-and-white photo. Cut sections from floral and striped patterned papers and rust-colored textured cardstock; mount on polka-dot patterned paper background. Mat photo on mustard-colored textured cardstock; mount. Cut cream-colored textured cardstock; mount index tab, layer with epoxy sticker and attach to mat with brads. Stamp word onto twill tape; attach to mat with straight pin. Embellish metal label holder with knotted ribbon; mount over letter tile on bottom of mat. Add silk flower and stitched button. Apply title with letter tiles and foam stamped letters.

*Cari Locken, Edmonton, Alberta, Canada*

**SUPPLIES:** Floral, striped and polka-dot patterned papers (Chatterbox); rust, mustard, and cream textured cardstock (Bazzill); index tab, concho (7 Gypsies); epoxy sticker (Creative Imaginations); letter stamps (PSX Design); label holder, silk flower, foam stamps (Making Memories); letter tiles (Westrim); brads; straight pin; ribbons; button

## The Truth

### INCORPORATE BOLD BLOCKED PATTERNS

Julie used brightly colored patterns to color block her background and complement her son's vibrant personality. Cut and punch strips, blocks and circles from patterned papers, green textured cardstock and white cardstock; layer all on light blue textured cardstock background. Affix punched circle-adorned envelope and photo on bottom of page. Journal on white cardstock; cut out and mat on green textured cardstock. Add patterned paper strip and paper clip; slide into envelope. Create title with letter stamps and a rub-on word applied to small block of white cardstock. Punch circle from patterned paper then cut in half and mount on edge of title block; add paper clip and mount in page corner.

*Julie Geiger, Gold Canyon, Arizona*

**SUPPLIES:** Patterned papers (KI Memories); light blue and green textured cardstocks (Bazzill); envelope (Ink It); letter stamps (PSX Design); rub-on words (Making Memories); circle punch (EK Success); rectangle punch (Marvy); white cardstock; staples

## Hannah

### HIGHLIGHT COLOR BLOCKS WITH RIBBON

Summer highlighted sections of her background with ribbon for a fun twist on color blocking. Ink edges of white cardstock background in green. Cut patterned paper sections and mount. Affix gingham ribbon along seams of patterned papers. Stitch photo onto page. Stamp title and journaling onto white sections. Lightly ink silk flowers in pink; affix. Stitch buttons with embroidery floss; mount in flower centers.

*Summer Ford, Bulverde, Texas*

**SUPPLIES:** Patterned paper (Provo Craft); letter stamps (Stampin' Up!); green and pink ink; white cardstock; gingham ribbon; floss; buttons

discover
r
Children, like animals, use all their senses to discover the world.
- Eudora Welty

# Discover

### ADD DIMENSION WITH LAYERS

Layered patterned papers in muted tones were used to complement black-and-white photos. Begin with two black cardstock backgrounds. Cut script patterned paper sections, gingham ribbon pieces and dark and light green textured cardstock sections and strips; layer all onto left and right pages aligning papers, ribbons and strips. On left page, mat black-and-white copy of photo on white cardstock; ink edges in black and mount. Cut desired section of color photo and mount over black-and-white photo with foam adhesive. Apply title with rub-on word. Cut striped patterned paper to fit square metal-rimmed tag; affix letter sticker and then mount piece on page. On right page, adhere black-and-white photocopies; affix cut-out piece of color photo on desired photo with foam adhesive. Journal on light green textured cardstock; cut out, ink edges in black and adorn with patterned paper strip. Mount piece on page.

*Cari Locken, Edmonton, Alberta, Canada*

**SUPPLIES:** Script patterned paper (7 Gypsies); dark and light green textured cardstocks (Bazzill); rub-on word and square metal-rimmed tag (Making Memories); striped patterned paper (Chatterbox); letter sticker (Me & My Big Ideas); black and white cardstocks; gingham ribbon; black ink; foam adhesive

# Sisters

### LAYER A PATTERNED PAPER BACKGROUND

Miki created a multilayered look without adding a lot of bulk using complementary-patterned papers. Begin with two patterned paper backgrounds; turn right page 180 degrees. On left page, cut a second patterned paper piece into small and large sections. Mount photo on larger section and wrap with charm-adorned ribbon. For tags, set eyelets in cardstock stickers, tie with fibers and attach to ribbon; add date with stickers. Mount on page with smaller cut patterned paper section. Apply title on smaller section with various letter stickers. On right page, create same photo mat and tags as before. Apply initials and date on tags with stickers. Cut smaller section from patterned paper and layer onto page with embellished photo mat. Apply sister poem onto cut section using various letter stickers and letter stamps.

*Miki Benedict, Modesto, California*
*Photos: Keith Benedict, Modesto, California*

**SUPPLIES:** Various patterned papers, cardstock tag stickers (Scrappy Cat); ribbon charms (Embelleez); various letter stickers (Creative Imaginations, Me & My Big Ideas); various letter stamps (Hero Arts, Ma Vinci's Reliquary); ribbon; eyelets; fibers

## Dare to Dream
### LAYER A MONOCHROMATIC BACKGROUND

Here Melanie used soft patterns stitched and layered at interesting angles as a backdrop for a sweet photo of her daughter. Cut section of polka-dot patterned paper, ink edges in brown and mount vertically, folding bottom left corner up on green patterned paper background; attach brad. Cut large section of floral patterned paper; machine stitch onto page. Adorn left edge with lace. Cut smaller section of polka-dot patterned paper; ink edges, adhere at an angle and add photo. Paint photo turn and brad white; attach over photo and add spiral clip. Paint three silver brads yellow and use to attach silk flowers on upper right corner of page. Add rickrack to top of page and preprinted ribbon to bottom of page, attaching with white brads. Apply title and journaling with rub-on words and letters. Wrap two pieces of fiber vertically around left side of page; tie in center.

*Melanie Douthit, West Monroe, Louisiana*

**SUPPLIES:** Polka-dot patterned paper (Chatterbox); green patterned paper and floral patterned paper (Sweetwater); photo turn, silk flowers, rub-on words and letters (Making Memories); spiral clip and preprinted ribbon (Creative Impressions); brown ink; white and silver brads; sewing machine; lace scrap; rickrack; white paint

## ...I Believe
### DISTRESS PATTERNED LAYERS

Diane exhibits a photo of her daughter with layers of inked and crumpled patterned papers that draw the eye. Print journaling on bottom of teal cardstock background. Ink edges in black. Cut sections of various patterned papers and ink all edges. Crumple large piece, flatten and layer onto page with remaining pieces. Mat photo on white cardstock; ink edges and mount.

*Diane Enarson, Corona, California*
*Lyrics: From Live's "Heaven"*

**SUPPLIES:** Patterned papers (KI Memories); teal cardstock; black ink

## Laughter
### LAYER TORN PAPERS

Angela made her layered background particularly appealing with torn patterned papers. Cut section of polka-dot patterned paper; tear top edge and mount on pink cardstock background. Cut photo mat from cream cardstock; tear bottom edge and add section of striped patterned paper across top. Mount photo and adhere to page. Cut strip from patterned paper; layer with strip of polka-dot patterned paper and mount along bottom of page. Print poem onto tag and ink in tan. Wrap page with cream and pink ribbons, hanging tag from knot. Apply rub-on word for title. Add small inked and date-stamped section of cream cardstock. Mount on bottom right corner of page. Embellish upper left and bottom right corners of page with brads.

*Angela Green, Georgetown, Illinois*

**SUPPLIES:** Polka-dot and striped patterned papers, date stamp, rub-on word (Making Memories); cream cardstock; cream and pink ribbons; tag; tan ink; brads

## Chocolate Chip Cookies
### LAYER PATTERNS, STRIPS AND BLOCKS

Cari's daughter loves chocolate, so in keeping with that theme she used rich brown layers for her background. Cut sections from various patterned papers, mesh paper, and strips from dark brown cardstock. Print title and journaling on tan cardstock. Cut out, ink in brown and layer all pieces onto background with photos and gingham ribbon. Add letter sticker to top of page. Cut circle from brown cardstock; stamp around edge in white ink. Cut circle from tan cardstock to fit metal-rimmed tag; ink in brown and adorn with stamped word and letter stickers. Stamp date on bottom of journaling box.

*Cari Locken, Edmonton, Alberta, Canada*

**SUPPLIES:** Taupe textured cardstock (DMD); various patterned papers (Creative Imaginations, 7 Gypsies); mesh paper (Magenta); letter stickers (Creative Imaginations, Sticker Studio); letter stamps (All Night Media, PSX Design); date stamp (Staples); brown and white ink; gingham ribbon; metal-rimmed circle tag

## Make Her Laugh
### TEAR A POCKET BACKGROUND

Angelia maximized her background space by creating a large torn pocket for her journaling and photo tags. Tear large diagonal section from red patterned paper and mount on denim patterned paper background to form pocket; machine stitch along edges. Cut section from striped patterned paper and mount vertically; layer with photos. Create one tag from a photo and the other from textured cream-colored cardstock with journaling; stitch buttons onto each and slip into pocket. Stitch along both sides of large definition sticker; mount onto pocket. Adhere additional definition stickers onto photo and upper right corner of page, accenting with a stitched button. Adhere metal letters to bottom right corner of page. Stamp portion of title on top of page. Cut squares from striped patterned paper and finish title by mounting letter tags over squares with mini brads.

*Angelia Wiggington, Belmont, Mississippi*

**SUPPLIES:** Red, denim, and striped patterned papers (Making Memories, 7 Gypsies); definitions, metal letters, letter tags (Making Memories); white textured cardstock (Bazzill); buttons (Junkitz); mini brads

## American Boy
### LAYER A TORN-STRIP BACKGROUND

Torn papers and cardstocks were layered and stitched for this appealing patriotic page. Tear sections of red and blue denim patterned papers and brown textured cardstocks; chalk one torn edge of each. Layer strips onto background cardstock, leaving center of one layer un-adhered to accommodate photo. Machine stitch along page border; ink edges in dark blue and red. Cut section from red denim patterned paper and mount at angle, tucking inside unglued strip; fold over one corner. Cut corner from blue denim patterned paper; cover folded corner and adhere. Mat photo on torn white cardstock; chalk edges and adhere, tucking inside unglued strip. Wrap fibers around bottom of layout; add metal star charm. Apply rub-on words for title. Stamp photo caption onto twill; attach with brads.

*Summer Ford, Bulverde, Texas*

**SUPPLIES:** Red and blue denim patterned papers (Karen Foster Design); brown textured cardstocks (Bazzill); metal star charm, rub-on words (Making Memories); letter stamps (Hero Arts, Stampin' Up!); chalk; red, dark blue and white inks; white cardstock; fibers; twill; brads

## Dish Boy Is 2 Cute
### LAYER PHOTOS ON TORN CARDSTOCK

Morag enhanced her background and created an eye-appealing photo mat with torn cardstock. Create page backgrounds from orange plaid patterned paper and blue textured cardstock. Print title on plaid patterned paper background, leaving room for ribbon. Print journaling on blue textured cardstock to accommodate photo, cut into a rectangle and accent with heart brad; affix ribbon across top of page and mount matted photo. Cut photo mats from black textured cardstock, red plaid patterned paper and orange textured cardstock; tear bottom edge from orange textured cardstock and accent with ribbon-tied token. Mount cropped photo on page over ribbon section. Stitch metal letter onto piece of ribbon; wrap frame and mount frame-cropped photo. For right page, cut large section from orange textured cardstock; tear top and bottom edges. Layer with orange plaid patterned paper section and conceal seams with charm-adorned ribbons. Mat preprinted mini tag on red plaid patterned paper and hang from bottom ribbon. Using a word processing program, resize a series of photos and place side by side in the document; print and cut out. Double mat on black textured cardstock and red plaid patterned paper; mount. Affix definition stickers above and below photo on page.

*Morag Mackay, Brandon, Manitoba, Canada*

**SUPPLIES:** Orange and red plaid patterned papers, orange textured cardstock (Chatterbox); blue and black textured cardstock (Bazzill); metal token (Pebbles); metal frame, metal letter, ribbon charms, definition stickers, preprinted mini tag (Making Memories); heart brad (Provo Craft); ribbon (Offray); word processing program (Microsoft)

## Perfection

### TEAR AND EMBOSS A BEACH SCENE

Here Becky created a beautiful and deceptively easy torn background. Journal on vellum; cut out and mount on left side of light blue textured cardstock background. Tear three sections from blue cardstock and one section from brown cardstock. Swipe embossing ink onto torn edges of the blue cardstock sections; cover in white embossing powder and heat to set. Layer embossed sections onto page with torn brown section. Cut netting to mat photo and adhere both to page. Cut smaller section of netting and adhere on bottom of page; adorn with metal charms and sea glass. Apply rub-on words to complete.

*Becky Thackston, Hiram, Georgia*

**SUPPLIES:** Light blue textured cardstock (Bazzill); rub-on words (Making Memories); embossing ink; white embossing powder; netting, charms, sea glass (www.Annalisse.com); vellum; blue and brown cardstocks

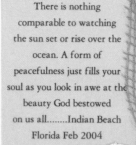

refresh

There is nothing comparable to watching the sun set or rise over the ocean. A form of peacefulness just fills your soul as you look in awe at the beauty God bestowed on us all........Indian Beach Florida Feb 2004

perfection

## Little Boy Blue

### TEAR A FAUX-PAINTED BACKGROUND

Becky tore a faux-painted patterned paper to give this background a rugged feel. Print journaling and first portion of title onto patterned paper; tear off bottom and mount on blue textured cardstock background. Stamp second part of title in blue using large block letter stamps. Adorn photo with decorative corners and adhere. Cut decorative metal strips and mount. Replace vellum in metal-rimmed tag with cardstock; add metal letter and adhere element on page. Finish with date stamp.

*Becky Thompson, Fruitland, Idaho*

**SUPPLIES:** Patterned paper (EK Success); blue textured cardstock background (Bazzill); decorative metal corners and strips, metal letter (Making Memories); large block letter stamps (Li'l Davis Designs); date stamp (Staples); blue ink; vellum metal-rimmed tag

*...each of us has one perfect partner who moves to the same secret music as our own.*

## *Perfect Partners*

### TEAR AND CHALK FOR A MARBLED EFFECT

Here Sharon's creative use of chalks on torn cardstock mimics the look of marble. Begin with two light purple textured cardstock backgrounds; print title and journaling on both. Tear two shades of purple textured cardstocks, chalking edges with charcoal color; layer on both pages. Using a pointed applicator, chalk marble lines on torn cardstocks pieces. Uniformly crop all photos along with one black cardstock piece; mat all on white cardstock and adhere. Embellish black cardstock piece with punch-out flower; add smaller flower to left page. Mat ribbon on white cardstock; adhere across both pages. Punch circles from white and black cardstocks and patterned paper; mount on bottom of right page next to ribbon.

*Sharon Whitehead, Vernon, British Columbia, Canada*

**SUPPLIES:** Light and dark purple textured cardstocks (Bazzill); charcoal chalk (Craf-T); punch-out flowers (Cropper Hopper); I Love You ribbon (Making Memories); patterned paper (7 Gypsies); circle punch (Marvy); chalk applicator; black and white cardstocks

## Fall '03

### STITCH A SPLIT BACKGROUND

Jane stitched patterned paper onto her background for added interest. Cut striped patterned paper to mount vertically on left side of orange textured cardstock background. Machine stitch along seam. Wrap gingham ribbon vertically around left side of page, adding pumpkin charm with blue and polka-dot ribbons. Triple mat photo on white, light blue and dark blue textured cardstocks; mount. Apply title on bottom of page with letter stickers. Mount fabric label on photo.

*Jane F. Ecker, Batavia, New York*

**SUPPLIES:** Striped patterned paper (Chatterbox); orange, white, light blue and dark blue textured cardstocks (Bazzill); pumpkin charm (source unknown); letter stickers (Creative Imaginations); fabric label (Me & My Big Ideas); ribbon

## My Boy

### STITCH A MIXED PATTERNED BACKGROUND

Here stitches added a crisp touch to a multipatterned background. Cut a section of striped paper and machine stitch it vertically onto circle patterned paper background. Journal on green textured cardstock; cut, leaving room for matted photo, title and embellishments. Accent with ribbon and adhere. Mat photo on brown cardstock, wrapping bottom with ribbon; mount on journaling box. Create title with letter stickers. Cut circles from cardstock and patterned papers to fit metal-rimmed tags. Add date and pen detail to smaller tag and mount over cardstock strip. Add letter sticker and pen detail to larger tag; layer over brown cardstock strip adhered over striped section.

*Cari Locken, Edmonton, Alberta, Canada*

**SUPPLIES:** Striped and circle patterned papers and letter sticker for tag (Chatterbox); green and tan textured cardstocks (Bazzill); letter stickers (Creative Imaginations); small and large metal-rimmed tags (Making Memories); green and brown ribbons; brown cardstock; black pen

## The Camera

### STITCH BACKGROUND STRIPS

Phillipa combined pretty patterned papers and cardstocks with stitching for an attractive background. Cut various sections of purple textured and non-textured cardstocks, pink cardstock and patterned papers; layer onto a white cardstock background until covered. Machine stitch each piece using different stitches. Journal on white cardstock; cut out and mount. Adorn select strips with buttons. Cut two page corners from purple cardstock and mount on top left and bottom right corners of page. Mat photos on purple textured and non-textured cardstocks; adhere. Cut photo corners from purple textured cardstock; mount on select corners of desired photos. Create title with letter stickers.

*Phillipa Campbell, Jerrabomberra, New South Wales, Australia*

**SUPPLIES:** Purple textured cardstock (Bazzill); patterned papers (Colorbök); letter stickers (Creative Imaginations); white, purple and pink cardstocks; buttons

## My Girl

### STITCH A PAGE BORDER

The stitching in Diana's background added a personal touch to premade embellishments. Cut sections of various patterned papers; stitch using color coordinating thread onto cardstock background, layering as desired. Mat photo on pink cardstock; add pink tab containing printed date on bottom right corner and mount. Round corners of title block and tag; affix title block. Journal on tag and mount on page. Adhere strip of patterned paper horizontally on page over tag; top off with tied ribbon.

*Diana Hudson, Bakersfield, California*

**SUPPLIES:** Patterned papers, title block, tag, pink tab (KI Memories); cardstock background; pink cardstock; corner rounder; ribbon

## Brothers

### LAYER A STRIPED BACKGROUND

Jenn enhanced a preprinted overlay with colorful strips of paper. Using a preprinted overlay as a guide, cut strips of yellow and orange cardstocks; mount accordingly onto red cardstock background. Mount photo on page, then overlay. Print journaling onto photo paper using black as the fill color and white for the font; once dry, mount atop overlay. Treat wood flower with red solvent ink; adorn with ribbon and mount on page.

*Jenn Brookover, San Antonio, Texas*

**SUPPLIES:** Preprinted overlay (Artistic Expressions); wood flower (Li'l Davis Designs); red solvent ink (Tsukineko); red, orange, and yellow cardstocks; photo paper; ribbon

## America

### TEAR PATRIOTIC STRIPS

Marianne captured a quintessential American moment in a patriotic layout with torn strips on a red background to mimic the American flag. Tear strips of white cardstock and stitch onto red cardstock background. Add blue buttons threaded with red fiber on each end. Stitch enlarged photo onto patterned paper mat; mount on page, forming a pocket behind it for journaling. Journal on white cardstock; mount on red cardstock piece. Stamp "slide up" onto ribbon and wrap around foam adhesive squares covered with blue cardstock; affix on top of tag for tag pull. Slide journaling behind photo. Affix laser-cut title on photo to finish.

*Marianne Dobbs, Alpena, Michigan*

**SUPPLIES:** Patterned paper (Club Scrap); letter stamps, sticky squares (Making Memories); laser-cut title (Photogenix); red and white cardstock; blue buttons; red fiber; ribbon

## That Beautiful Smile...

### INCORPORATE SOLID AND PATTERNED BACKGROUND STRIPS

Rebecca chose a pretty but subdued background of cut strips to complement black-and-white photos of her little girl. Begin with two light green cardstock backgrounds; print date on left page and journaling on right page. Cut various strips from white and green cardstocks and pink patterned paper; mount across center of backgrounds. For left page, mat enlarged photo onto white cardstock and mount. Adorn left page corner with buttons. For right page, adhere photos side by side on white cardstock mat and mount. Adorn bottom right corner with buttons.

*Rebecca Cooper, Raymond, Alberta, Canada*
*Photos: K. Merrill Photography, Raymond, Alberta, Canada*

**SUPPLIES:** Pink patterned paper (Masterpiece Studios); light green, green, and white cardstocks; buttons

## Pocket Full of Rainbows

### ADD COORDINATING BRADS TO CARDSTOCK STRIPS

Kimberly created a vivid background with colorful cardstock strips. Cut multicolored textured and non-textured cardstock strips; ink edges in black and attach to black cardstock background with coordinating colored brads. Cut section of corrugated paper; lightly ink edges in black and mount. Layer with photo. Cut or punch circle from white cardstock; edge in black. Cut slivers from all cardstocks; mount on circle. Cut rectangle title block from white cardstock; ink edges and adhere, mounting circle on left side of block. Apply portion of title with letter stickers. Stamp remainder of title on white cardstock; cut out, ink edges and adhere to title block with foam tape.

*Kimberly Kesti, Phoenix, Arizona*

**SUPPLIES:** Various colored textured cardstocks (Bazzill); letter stickers (KI Memories); letter stamps (PSX Design); various colored non-textured cardstocks; various colored brads; black ink; corrugated paper; foam adhesive

# Outside
### CREATE A PATTERNED BACKGROUND WITH CLIP ART

Here Nancy arranged watermark-style clip art for a custom background. Using a digital imaging program, print snowflake clip art for a watermark effect onto a purple cardstock background. Apply title to top of page with vellum letter stickers. Cut patterned paper section and adhere along bottom of page; mount page pebble over select word. Affix photo on left side of page; apply rub-on sentence along bottom and add decorative brad. Print title and journaling on transparency. Cut out title and adhere on top of page over stickers; cut out journaling and mount next to photo. Cut thin strip from yellow cardstock; affix across page over edges of transparencies. Stamp month under journaling. Border photo and journaling block with ribbon. Add snowflake brad to photo. Using label maker, print date; affix on ribbon under label holder; accent with ribbon.

*Nancy Lahman, Algonquin, Illinois*

**SUPPLIES:** Digital imaging program (Microsoft); vellum letter stickers (Mrs. Grossman's); patterned paper (Karen Foster Design); page pebble, rub-on sentence, date stamp, decorative brad (Making Memories); label holder (source unknown); label maker (Dymo); purple cardstock; transparency; yellow cardstock; ribbons

# Determination
### PRINT DIRECTLY ONTO A BACKGROUND

For a crisp-looking, quick and easy background, J.J. printed her title and its definition directly onto her background page. Print title on bottom of sienna cardstock background. Print journaling and title definition on peach cardstock; cut and mount over top half of background page. Adhere photo on right side of page; adorn with photo turn attached with brad. Affix ribbon along paper seams and tie into bow.

*J.J. Killins, Redondo Beach, California*

**SUPPLIES:** Photo turn (7 Gypsies); sienna and peach cardstocks; ribbon

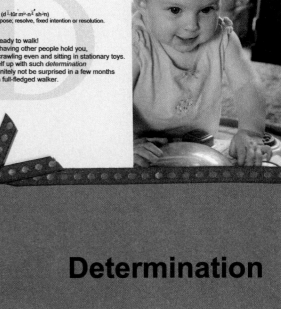

## Happy Harvest Memories

### INK SQUARES FOR DEPTH

Inked patterned paper squares accented with ribbon made for both an easy and artistic page background. Cut or punch squares from patterned papers; ink edges brown. Set eyelets in select squares and tie with sheer ribbon. Assemble and mount on brown textured cardstock background. Mat photo on cream-colored textured cardstock and mount. Apply rub-on word above photo. Cut strip of cream-colored textured cardstock; ink in brown and staple at top of page. Print label for portion of title; affix across inked strip. Stamp caption onto cream-colored textured cardstock; cut out, ink edges in brown and staple onto bottom left corner of page. Using lettering stencil, cut remainder of title from cream-colored textured cardstock and adhere.

*Stephanie Carpenter, Sandusky, Ohio*

**SUPPLIES:** Patterned papers (Scenic Route Paper Co.); brown and cream-colored textured cardstocks (Bazzill); rub-on word (Making Memories); labels (Dymo); letter stamps (Hero Arts); lettering stencil (Wordsworth); brown ink; eyelets; sheer ribbon; stapler

## Water

### ADD WHIMSICAL BACKGROUND CIRCLES

Debbie used handcut, arbitrarily placed circles to enhance her background. Mount a large cut section of light blue cardstock over a slightly larger textured white cardstock section; layer vertically onto teal cardstock background. Using circle cutter, cut circles from light blue and teal cardstocks; cut select circles in half and mount all on page. Create title with die-cut letters and apply vertically along white edge. Cut section of patterned paper and mat on white cardstock; adhere across center of page. Mat photo on white cardstock and affix. Apply rub-on flowers and letters onto acrylic bauble and affix on patterned paper piece. Apply name vertically next to photo with rub-on letters.

*Debbie Hill, Westford, Massachusetts*

**SUPPLIES:** White textured cardstock (Bazzill); circle cutter (Provo Craft); acrylic bauble (Junkitz); die-cut letters (QuicKutz); patterned paper (source unknown); rub-on flowers (American Traditional Designs); rub-on letters (Autumn Leaves); light blue, teal and white cardstocks

## *All My Devotion*

### SOFTEN A BACKGROUND WITH PAINT

Sanding and paint detail artfully enhance the background of Kimberly's layout. Cut striped patterned paper in half and mount on light purple cardstock background. Lightly sand patterned paper; paint edge of page in white. Once dry, ink lightly in purple. Wrap green ribbon across center of page; tie on right side and machine stitch onto page along right side. Sand edges of photo, mat on white cardstock, layer onto polka-dot mat and adhere on page. Machine stitch bottom of photo mat. Add white paint detail; layer with metal letters. Paint stitched tin tile white and adorn with bottle cap. Attach on page with brads. Stamp numbers on bottom of page; cover desired number with page pebble.

*Kimberly Kesti, Phoenix, Arizona*

**SUPPLIES:** Striped patterned paper (Scrapworks); polka-dot patterned paper (Provo Craft); metal letters, stitched tin tile, page pebble (Making Memories); bottle cap (Li'l Davis Designs); number stamps (PostModern Design); light purple and white cardstocks; sandpaper; white paint; purple ink; green ribbon; brads

## *Forever*

### PAINT A CANVASLIKE BACKGROUND

Danielle used a simple painting technique in pastels to give her background a soft feel and to perfectly match her patterned papers. Begin with white textured cardstock background; paint sections of page in pastel blue and purple. Mount cut sections of patterned paper where desired; highlight exposed painted areas with a dry brush in white. Once dry, print journaling onto page and affix ribbon to line sections. Mat photo on black cardstock; adhere on page along with definition stickers.

*Danielle Layton, Clarksville, Tennessee*

**SUPPLIES:** White textured cardstock background (Bazzill); pastel blue, purple and white paints, definition stickers (Making Memories); patterned paper (K & Company); ribbon; black cardstock

## Art Is Love
### USE LARGE STAMPS FOR BACKGROUNDS

Here Becky demonstrated how large stamps can lend a hand in making custom backgrounds when used on an entire page. Begin by stamping phrase stamp in oregano-colored ink onto white textured cardstock; tear diagonally and chalk torn edge. Print journaling onto oregano-colored textured cardstock; mount torn piece on top, attaching brad on upper left corner. Adhere photo atop two copper tags turned vertically. Attach another copper tag along bottom of page, stamping expression with black ink.

*Becky Thompson, Fruitland, Idaho*

**SUPPLIES:** White and oregano-colored textured cardstocks (Bazzill); "Art Is Life & Beauty" stamp (Hero Arts); copper tags (www.twopeasinabucket .com); "Art Is Love" expression stamp (PSX Design); black solvent ink (Tsukineko); oregano-colored ink; chalk; brad

## Discover...
### STAMP A SUBTLE THEMED BACKGROUND

This seasonal layout was enhanced with an autumn-inspired stamped background. Begin by stamping leaf image onto brown textured cardstock background with watermark ink. Double mat photo onto light and dark brown cardstocks; affix on page, adding cork letter stickers on top of photo. Cut strips of fabric; mount, adding decorative brads. Ink title tag in brown and add definition; complete with cork letter stickers, metal letters and fibers. Tie off and mount. Print journaling on tan cardstock; cut out, ink edges and mat on brown cardstock. Punch holes for fiber; tie off, wrapping ends around decorative brad.

*Stacey Irene Wakelin, Surrey, British Columbia, Canada*

**SUPPLIES:** Brown textured cardstock background (Bazzill); leaf stamp (PSX Design); watermark ink (Tsukineko); decorative brads, metal letters, definition (Making Memories); cork letter stickers (Creative Imaginations); light and dark brown and tan cardstocks; fabric; brown ink; fibers

# CHAPTER THREE
## *titles, borders, mats*

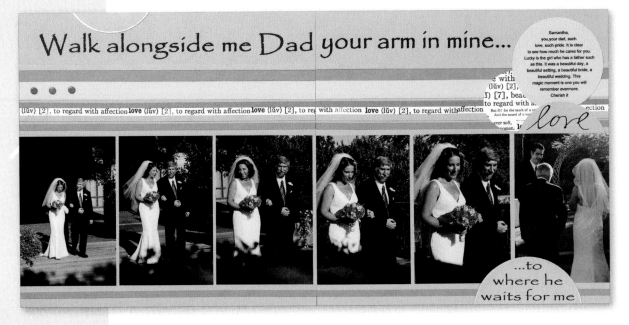

## Walk Alongside Me Dad

### PRINT A TITLE ACROSS A SPREAD

For an easy and eye-catching treatment, Sharon printed her title directly onto both of her background pages. Begin by printing title directly onto two light green textured cardstock backgrounds. Cut various-sized strips from shades of green and purple textured cardstocks along with patterned paper strip; mount on pages, embellishing with brads. Adhere photos to pages. Print journaling in circle and sub-title in half-circle formats; cut from purple and green textured cardstocks, outlining subtitle with silver leafing pen and adding rub-on word to other half-circle. Cut patterned paper circle and mount all on page.

*Sharon Whitehead, Vernon, British Columbia, Canada*

**SUPPLIES:** Green and purple textured cardstocks (Bazzill); patterned paper (7 Gypsies); rub-on word (Making Memories); silver leafing pen (Krylon); brads

## At the Pool

### PRINT A TITLE USING A FUN COMPUTER FONT

Just-right fonts are imperative for fun titles, and Tracy's made a big splash. Begin by cropping photos. Cut sections of various patterned papers and layer over black cardstock background page, surrounding cropped photos; mount all on page. Cut larger section of patterned paper for focal photo; mat on white cardstock and affix on page. Print title onto white cardstock strip, leaving space for matted photo; mount across page. Journal on white cardstock; adhere onto patterned paper section. Embellish page with word punch-outs covered with colored conchos.

*Tracy Miller, Fallston, Maryland*

**SUPPLIES:** Patterned papers (Doodlebug Design); word punch-outs, colored conchos (Scrapworks); black and white cardstocks

## I'm a Big Sister
### COMBINE SEVERAL STICKER STYLES

By adding a stamped pattern to select letter stickers, Janetta added instant pizazz to her page. Cut section of patterned paper; adhere across center of red textured cardstock background page, mounting photos on top. Adhere photo corners cut from cream cardstock on opposite corners of page; adorn with cherry embellishments. Journal on cream cardstock; mount. Stamp flower pattern in red ink onto desired letter stickers; stamp same pattern onto white cardstock and cut into shape of dress to personalize premade wire girl sticker. Mat stamped letter sticker on black cardstock; cut out with craft knife and affix along with other letter stickers to complete title.

*Janetta Abucejo Wieneke, Memory Makers Books*
*Photos: Jonathan Abucejo, Copley, Ohio*

**SUPPLIES:** Patterned paper (K & Company); red textured cardstock background (Bazzill); cherry embellishments (Creative Imaginations); flower stamp (Hero Arts); various letter stickers (American Crafts, EK Success, Wordsworth); girl and baby sticker (Me & My Big Ideas); cream, white, and black cardstocks; red ink; wire; foam tape

## ...Shadow
### CRAFT A STICKER AND STAMP TITLE

A variety of letter stickers combined with stamps made La'Shea's title both quick and visually interesting. Journal on blue patterned paper; cut out and mount over top half of green cardstock background. Adhere photo to page. Cut strips from green and orange cardstocks to flank photo. Stamp portion of title on bottom of page with foam stamps and orange paint. Apply remainder of title with various letter stickers onto cardstock strips and on die-cut squares. Stamp date on bottom of page.

*La'Shea Lowe-Parker, Starkville, Mississippi*

**SUPPLIES:** Blue patterned paper, various letter stickers, die-cut squares (KI Memories); foam stamps, date stamp (Making Memories); green and orange cardstocks; orange paint

## ...Laugh
### CREATE A TITLE WITH STAMPED TAGS

Christine used letter stamps to create customized tags for a title. Cut strip from white cardstock and adhere on patterned paper background, attaching brad on left side. Enlarge photo and mount. Print portion of title on white cardstock; cut into strip and mount across top of page, attaching brad on left side. Stamp remainder of title on yellow cardstock; cut to fit metal-rimmed tags. Attach tags to white strip with brads. Print quote on transparency; cut out and adhere. Mat small black-and-white copy of photo on black cardstock. Cut card for journaling from white cardstock; adhere matted photo on top. Cover photo with transparency. Make "open" tab from white cardstock; affix on inside flap. Write photo details on yellow cardstock; cut to fit label holder. Mount with brads.

*Christine Brown, Hanover, Minnesota*

**SUPPLIES:** Patterned paper (Karen Foster Design); letter stamps (Wordsworth); metal-rimmed rectangle tags (Making Memories); white, yellow and black cardstocks; brads; transparency; label holder

## Trick or Treat
### FEATURE A PREPRINTED TAG TITLE

Preprinted themed tags made Jennifer's title easy to apply as well as eye-pleasing. Mount cut section of black cardstock vertically down center of orange textured cardstock background page. Cut kraft-colored paper with precut windows in half; ink inside edges, tie ribbons and muslin pieces onto bottom of left piece and mount photos. Journal onto orange textured cardstock; cut into strips, ink edges and attach to page with floss stitching. For title, tie sections of ribbon and muslin together and string tags; mount to finish.

*Jennifer Bertsch, Tallahassee, Florida*

**SUPPLIES:** Orange textured cardstock (Bazzill); precut window paper (unknown); date stamp (Making Memories); title tags (Li'l Davis Designs); black cardstock; brown ink; ribbon; muslin pieces; floss

## Friends

### PRINT YOUR TITLE ON PATTERNED PAPER

Suzy printed her title in an artistic arrangement on a patterned background. Enlarge photo and mount on a background page. Arrange and print title on patterned paper to cover remainder of background; mount on page. Journal on white cardstock and cut into strips; ink edges in brown and mount near top right corner of page. Adorn journaling with brads and spiral clip. Set eyelets on bottom right corner of photo. Run various ribbons through eyelets and tie into knots.

*Suzy West, Fremont, California*

**SUPPLIES:** Patterned paper (Basic Grey); spiral clip (Making Memories); white cardstock; brown ink; brads

## Relax

### STAMP A TWILL RIBBON TITLE

Samuel stamped twill tape for a quick and clever page title. Layer a dark brown textured cardstock background with sections of patterned paper. Mat photos on white cardstock. Cut sections and strips from mesh; layer onto page with matted photos. Stamp title in black onto pre-embellished twill tape with letter stamps; mount over patterned paper strip. Stamp windmill image onto paper envelope; layer with mesh section and adhere. Journal on tag; ink edges, set eyelet, add twine and slip into envelope. Adorn focal photo with metal word charm mounted over mesh. Stamp date in upper left corner.

*Samuel Cole, Stillwater, Minnesota*

**SUPPLIES:** Plaid patterned paper (Chatterbox); dark brown textured cardstock (Bazzill); patterned papers (Mustard Moon, PSX Design, Rocky Mountain Scrapbook Co.); mesh (Magic Mesh); letter stamps (All Night Media); pre-embellished twill tape (EK Success); tag in a bag (DMD); windmill stamp (Creative Impressions); metal word charm (Darice); black ink; eyelet; twine

## Portrait of a Boy

### FEATURE A STICKER TITLE ON A STICKER LABEL

Elizabeth made use of the various stickers to form an easy yet artful title. Mat rust-colored patterned paper on a brown textured cardstock background. Make copies of photos; tear into sections and layer select sections over intact originals. Double mat photos on brown and tan textured cardstocks, adhering photo corner on one corner of each photo; mount. Journal on tan textured cardstock; cut out, then tear off bottom edge. Mount cut blue cardstock section beneath torn journaling element; mount. Add blue and antique brads. Affix large oval sticker on top right corner of page; apply title with various letter stickers. Cut twill tape sections and stitch onto title over top edge of page; accent with brads.

*Elizabeth Ruuska, Rensselaer, Indiana*

**SUPPLIES:** Rust-colored patterned paper (Design Originals); brown textured cardstock (Bazzill); tan textured cardstock (Club Scrap); photo corners (Close To My Heart); large oval sticker (Sticker Studio); letter stickers (Doodlebug Design, Me & My Big Ideas); blue cardstock; blue and antique brads; twill tape

## Get Your Game On

### CREATE A COLLAGED STICKER TITLE

Various stickers and dimensional accents add to the rugged appeal of Jill's preprinted title. Layer a patterned paper background with a preprinted title and large section of patterned paper. Add photo double-matted on patterned papers; accent with molding strip and stickers. Vertically assemble elements cut from patterned papers, stickers, a paint- and ink-treated stencil, wood letter tiles and circles; add paint-treated photo turns.

*Jill Jackson-Mills, Roswell, Georgia*
*Photo: Photography by David, Roswell, Georgia*

**SUPPLIES:** Patterned papers (Mustard Moon, Sticker Studio); stickers (Me & My Big Ideas, Sticker Studio, Wordsworth); wood tile letters (source unknown); wood circle letters (Li'l Davis Designs); molding strip (unknown); photo turns, stencil, gold and white acrylic paints

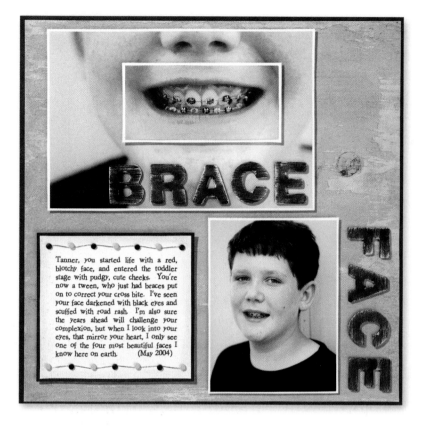

## Brace Face
### COLORIZE WOODEN LETTERS

Denise painted the wood letters for her title but saved time by using painted wood-patterned background paper. Trim and mat patterned paper on black cardstock background. Enlarge and print double of focal photo; cut out desired area from copy. Mat all photos on white cardstock; adhere all on page, layering larger photo and cropped photo onto page with foam adhesive. Journal on cream cardstock; color edges with colored pencils and mat on black cardstock. Embellish with brads and wire to mimic braces; mount on page. Paint wood letters in blue, then with black pigment powder. When dry, apply white paint using a dry brush technique; mount letters onto photo and page.

*Denise Tucker, Versailles, Indiana*

**SUPPLIES:** Painted wood patterned paper (Pebbles); colored pencils (Staedtler); wood letters (Plaid); pigment powder (AMACO); black and cream cardstocks; foam adhesive; wire; brads; blue and white paints

Tanner, you started life with a red, blotchy face, and entered the toddler stage with pudgy, cute cheeks. You're now a tween, who just had braces put on to correct your cross bite. I've seen your face darkened with black eyes and scuffed with road rash. I'm also sure the years ahead will challenge your complexion, but when I look into your eyes, that mirror your heart, I only see one of the four most beautiful faces I know here on earth. (May 2004)

## Bare Baby
### PAINT A LETTER STENCIL TITLE

Rhonda vertically mounted her painted letter stencils for an eye-catching title. Start with a floral patterned paper background. Mat photo on pink linen patterned paper and adhere to page; adorn with photo turns attached with brads. Paint letter stencils green; mount cut sections of white floral patterned papers beneath stencils and adhere to page. Attach paper flowers to page with heart-shaped brads. Complete title with rub-on letters.

*Rhonda Jones, Aloha, Oregon*
*Photo: Erin Ungewitter, Portland, Oregon*

**SUPPLIES:** Pink and white floral, pink striped and pink linen patterned papers (Chatterbox); letter stencils (Autumn Leaves); paper flowers, heart brads, rub-on letters (Making Memories); photo turns (7 Gypsies); green paint; brads

## *New Beginnings*

### CREATE A TITLE WITH RUB-ON WORDS

Here rub-on words form a page title, all the while offering artful contrast to black-and-white photos. Apply a strip of slate-colored cardstock across a black cardstock background. Mat an enlarged photo printed with a white border with slate and white cardstocks. Print passage-style journaling on white cardstock and adhere to right side of background. Cut a panel from black cardstock. Layer with a cropped printed transparency mounted over white cardstock. Add cropped panoramic photo accented with rub-on word to other side. Layer panel over journaling by attaching to page with three cardstock hinges affixed with glue dots.

*Emily Curry Hitchingham, Memory Makers Books*

**SUPPLIES:** Rub-on words (Making Memories); printed transparency (Club Scrap); black, white and slate-colored cardstocks

## July 4

### CUT A COMPUTER FONT TITLE

Leah used a computer font as a guide for cutting out her quick and easy title, and enhanced it with embellished die-cut fireworks. Begin by cutting out large, medium and small circles from blue, white and red cardstocks. Affix fireworks die cuts on circle mats opposite their color; add sequins and mount. Journal on white cardstock; mat onto blue cardstock and cut into circle. Mount on page with right and bottom of circle hanging off edge; trim excess. Mat photo on red cardstock and adhere. Using computer font as a guide, cut out title from red and blue cardstocks and mount on page to complete.

*Leah Blanco Williams, Rochester, New York*

**SUPPLIES:** Fireworks die cuts (Deluxe Designs); blue, white, red and black cardstocks; sequins

## Create, Fun, Imagine
### UTILIZE A PAPER PATTERN FOR A BORDER

Employing creative photo placement on patterned paper created an instant border for Anna's two-page spread. Begin with two patterned paper backgrounds; ink edges in black. For left page, turn paper so that squares are on bottom; adhere photos. Apply rub-on words to desired squares along with metal letter. Cut square from blue cardstock to fit metal-rimmed tag; adorn with acrylic charm and mount. On right page, turn background so squares are on the left; apply rub-on words to select squares. Mount photos. Cut green cardstock square to fit metal-rimmed tag; affix acrylic charm and mount. Cut oval from striped patterned paper to fit metal-rimmed tag; adorn with metal word. Cut slits in tag and thread ribbon through; wrap remaining ribbon vertically on right side of page, securing from behind.

*Anna M. Burgess, Clarksville, Tennessee*

**SUPPLIES:** Patterned papers (SEI); rub-on words, metal words and square and oval metal-rimmed tags (Making Memories); acrylic charms (Doodlebug Design); black ink; blue and green cardstocks; ribbon

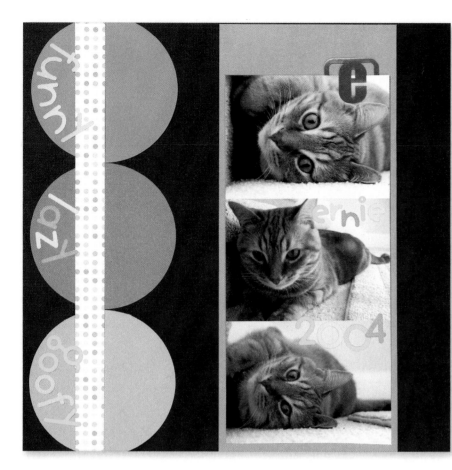

## Ernie 2004
### CREATE A PLAYFUL PATTERNED BORDER

Katy wanted a layout that reflects her cat's frisky nature so she created a fun circle border layered with a patterned paper strip. Mat photos vertically on gray cardstock strip, affixing letter clip over top photo; mount on black textured cardstock background. Cut circles from blue, orange and green textured cardstocks; mount vertically on left side of page. Cut strip of polka-dot patterned paper and mount over cardstock circles. Apply letter stickers onto photo and circles for title.

*Katy Jurasevich, Crown Point, Indiana*

**SUPPLIES:** Black, blue, orange, and green textured cardstocks (Bazzill); letter clip (Scrapworks); polka-dot patterned paper, letter stickers (KI Memories); gray cardstock

## 42x38
### PLAY UP A PATTERNED BORDER

Kelli found she had a ready-made border on her whimsical patterned paper background. Print title and journaling on right side of background. Mat photo on brown cardstock and adhere. Affix label sticker across bottom of page. Print photo caption on blue cardstock; cut out, affix under slide mount and over label sticker.

*Kelli Lawlor, Norfolk, Virginia*

**SUPPLIES:** Patterned paper (SEI); label maker (Dymo); slide mount (Magic Scraps); brown and blue cardstocks

## Caeden and Dalton

### CRAFT A PUNCHED SQUARE BORDER

Kristin's quick border was achieved with enhanced cut-out squares. Start with two green patterned paper backgrounds. Add solid and patterned papers to left page and punched and inked squares to each page. Cut enlarged photo into two sections and mount across pages. Cut patterned paper strips for photo border. Create title block and caption in a word processing program by making a text box, filling with black, applying white text and printing. Cut into square and strip elements and round corners of each. Attach square conchos over words in title block and add letter beads to caption strip. Mount block to left page and cut caption to span both pages. Journal on bottom of left page. Add black punched circle accented with concho to bottom of right page. Handwrite date to complete.

*Kristin Holly, Glendale, Arizona*

**SUPPLIES:** Green, blue striped and green striped patterned papers, cut-out squares, square and circle conchos (Scrapworks); letter beads (Westrim); word processing program (Microsoft); black ink; corner rounder; brads; circle punch; black cardstock

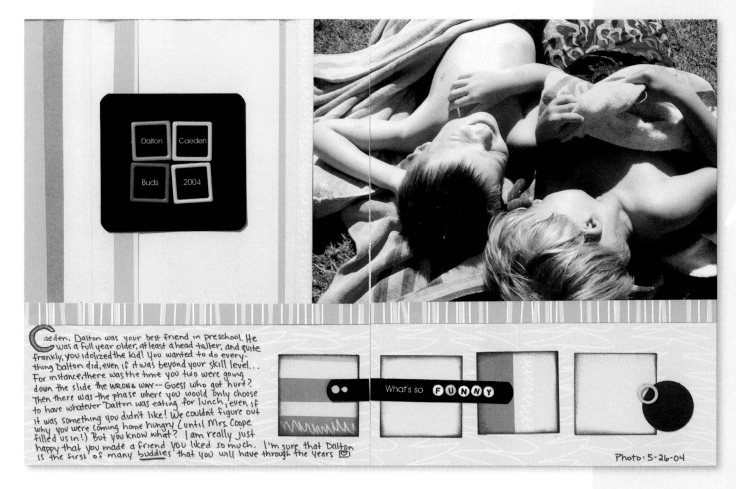

## Happy Boy
### STRING A PUNCH-OUT BORDER

Cara formulated her fun border with fibers and punch-out shape elements. Cut sections from striped and floral patterned papers; layer over white textured cardstock background. Mount unmatted and white cardstock-matted photo to page. String punch-outs vertically along right side of page with fibers. Affix die-cut squares on top of punch-outs with foam adhesive; mount letter sticker on top of small square. Add additional die-cut accents to page corner. Apply title with letter stickers and handwrite date beneath photo.

*Cara Vincens, Thionville, France*

**SUPPLIES:** Striped and floral patterned papers, die cuts, punch-outs (KI Memories); white textured cardstock (Bazzill); letter sticker for die-cut square (Creative Memories); letter stickers for title (Creative Imaginations); white cardstock; fibers; foam adhesive

## ...The Perfect Pumpkin
### CREATE A MULTISHAPE BORDER

This bold and colorful border was created by combining various preprinted squares, an acrylic square and a circle metal-rimmed tag. Cut various pieces of patterned paper and green textured cardstock; ink edges in black and adhere all on a cardstock background. Ink edges of preprinted punch-out squares, then mat onto inked tan cardstock mats; apply down left side of page, mounting clear pocket after first square. Apply title on squares with letter stickers, letter stamps and metal letters. Adorn last two squares with brads and acrylic square. Finish title with letter stickers affixed on punched and inked circles mounted on circle tag; tie off tag with gingham ribbon and slip into clear pocket. Wrap striped ribbon around photo, hanging tag with stamped date; layer onto page with inked paint chip. Stamp journaling onto page. Color pumpkins in photos with photo coloring pens to finish.

*Stacey Kingman, Ellsworth, Illinois*

**SUPPLIES:** Various patterned papers, preprinted paper squares, acrylic square (KI Memories); green textured cardstock (Bazzill); letter stickers (Creative Imaginations, KI Memories); letter and date stamps (Making Memories); circle punch (Family Treasures); photo pens (EK Success); black ink; tan cardstock; brads; circle tags; gingham ribbon; striped ribbon

## Chores at 2
### CREATE A BORDER OF TUCKED-AWAY TAGS

Jennifer assigned her corrugated border double duty by using it as a pocket for journaling tags. Cut section of corrugated cardstock; alter with green paint. Mount on right side of green textured cardstock background along three sides only to accommodate tags. Cut section from cream-colored textured cardstock; mount at askew angle, trimming corners. Mat photo on blue textured cardstock; mount with foam adhesive. Accent with ribbon and tag-adorned spiral clip. Cut section from pink textured cardstock; tear off top edge and stamp portion of title using foam stamps. Complete title with a painted metal number and your own handwriting. Add flower embellished with spiral clip, ribbon and button. Cut tags from cream textured cardstock; staple ribbons onto ends of each. Journal on tags and slide each into corrugated border.

*Jennifer Kotas, Poughkeepsie, New York*

**SUPPLIES:** Corrugated cardstock (Paper Source); spiral clip, foam stamps, metal letter (Making Memories); silk flower (Michaels); green paint; foam adhesive; mini tags; floss; ribbons; button

## Zack And Mack
### ARRANGE TAG RUB-ONS FOR AN ARTSY BORDER

Katherine crafted a fun and colorful border using tag rub-ons in an all-new way. Print title and journaling onto right side of spruce-colored cardstock background. Print dingbat character onto bottom right corner. Apply rub-on border by cutting out circles and half circles and rubbing onto background page to form a vertical border. Layer with smaller rub-on circles. Apply rub-ons near dingbat and embellish with brads. Mount photos on left side of page.

*Katherine Teague, New Westminster, British Columbia, Canada*

**SUPPLIES:** Tag rub-ons (Creative Imaginations); spruce cardstock; brads

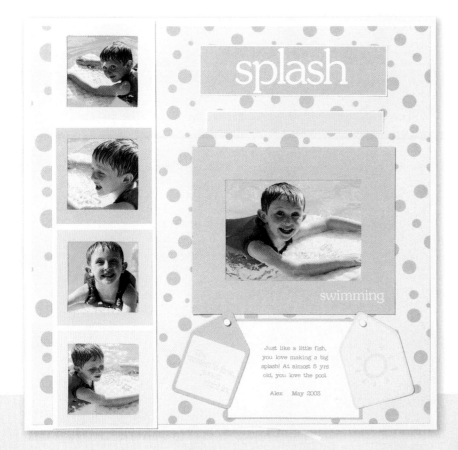

## Splash

### UTILIZE PREMADE PHOTO BORDERS

A premade photo border strip allowed Jlyne to incorporate additional photos as well as enhance her design. Mat patterned paper on a white cardstock background. Crop photos and mount onto page under border strip along left side of page. Adhere focal photo to center of page and layer with printed frame. Adhere premade title and green strip above focal photo. Journal onto premade journaling box and mount. Attach premade tags to journaling block with brads.

*Jlyne Hanback, Biloxi, Mississippi*

**SUPPLIES:** Patterned paper, premade photo border, frame, title, green strip, journaling box and tags (My Mind's Eye); white cardstock; brads

## Bobbi Brown

### STACK A STRIKING PHOTO BORDER

Kelli used photos from an encounter with renowned makeup artist Bobbi Brown as a border for her layout. Cut shopping bag with name/logo for title; mount on black cardstock background. Adhere enlarged photo below title and cropped photos down left edge of page for border. Journal on white cardstock, leaving room for focal photo. Mount photo on journaling block, then adhere to page with foam adhesive.

*Kelli Noto, Centennial, Colorado*

**SUPPLIES:** Shopping bag; black cardstock background; white cardstock; foam adhesive

## Annual Friends Cruise

### STAMP A BORDER WITH PAINT

Jeniece painted a border for a quick and easy page that adds an elegant touch. Cut one large and three small circles from patterned paper; paint edges in black and mount on patterned paper background. Stamp border using black paint and foam stamp. Edge file folder with paint, then journal, adding rub-on words and labels for date and title. Mount on page, adding black twine to tie closed. Mat photo on black cardstock; attach on page with large brads. Apply title with letter stickers and plastic letters.

*Jeniece Higgins, Lake Forest, Illinois*

**SUPPLIES:** Patterned papers (Basic Grey); foam stamp, rub-on words (Making Memories); file folder (Rusty Pickle); labels (Dymo); letter stickers (Provo Craft); plastic letters (Creative Imaginations); black paint; black twine; black cardstock; brads

## Back-to-School Shoes

### PAINT A METAL BORDER

Paint and ink were used to alter metal strips for a unique border. Trim and mat patterned paper onto black cardstock background. Adhere series of photos side by side along bottom. Paint metal strips with cream acrylic paint. When dry, ink with black and mount on page. Mat focal photo on white cardstock; adhere with foam adhesive. Journal on yellow patterned paper; cut into square and attach small section of ruler patterned paper with eyelets. Ink edges of journaling piece, add shoelace through eyelets and mount with foam adhesive. Apply title with labels and letter stickers.

*Denise Tucker, Versailles, Indiana*

**SUPPLIES:** Patterned paper (Rusty Pickle); metal strips (Making Memories); yellow and ruler patterned papers (Basic Grey); labels (Dymo); letter stickers (EK Success); black and white cardstocks; cream acrylic paint; black ink; foam adhesive; eyelets; shoelace

## Friends

### STACK PREPRINTED RIBBONS FOR A BORDER

Gayle used a variety of preprinted ribbons to form a pretty border. Cut mat from textured green cardstock for enlarged photo; ink edges in black. Cut tab from "friend" synonym tab; ink in black and adhere on top and backside of photo; machine stitch photo onto mat, then mount on yellow textured cardstock background. Stamp date on bottom right corner of photo. Wrap ribbons adorned with ribbon charms around bottom of page; secure on back of page. Ink edges of page in black. Stamp title with letter stamps. Attach paper flowers with brad. Journal on green textured cardstock; cut out and adhere on bottom left corner of page. For journal cover, ink edges of "friend" synonym tab and attach hinge on left side. Mount over journaling, using spiral clip to keep closed.

*Gayle Hodgins, Philadelphia, Pennsylvania*

**SUPPLIES:** Green and yellow textured cardstocks (Bazzill); "friend" synonym tab (Autumn Leaves); date stamp (Staples); word and polka-dot ribbons (Creative Imaginations, Lifetime Moments, Li'l Davis Designs, Making Memories); ribbon charms, hinge, paper flowers, spiral clip (Making Memories); letter stamps (MoBe' Stamps!); black ink; brad

## In the Middle

### CREATE A PREPRINTED TRANSPARENCY BORDER

A preprinted transparency provided the perfect subtle border for Rhonda's design. Print sentiment on green patterned paper, omitting last word; cut out and mount on striped patterned paper background. Add last word with acrylic letter stickers. Cut section of red flower patterned paper; mount. Cut strips of faux-linen patterned paper, mounting one on upper right corner and one on bottom left corner of page. Attach preprinted transparency to page with brads along the linen strips. Journal on green patterned paper; cut out and adhere. Mat focal photo on red linen patterned paper and adhere along with unmatted photo. Accent page with woven label and silk flower.

*Rhonda Jones, Aloha, Oregon*
*Photos: Erin Ungewitter, Portland, Oregon*

**SUPPLIES:** Preprinted transparency (Sweetwater); patterned papers (Chatterbox, Sweetwater); acrylic letter stickers (K & Company); silk flower (Michaels); woven label (Li'l Davis Designs); brads

## It's Because of You
### TEAR AND ROLL A PHOTO MAT

Diane artistically enhanced her photo with a torn and rolled patterned paper mat. Cut sections of brown polka-dot and brown striped patterned papers; mount on a light blue textured cardstock background. Print quote on transparency; cut out and mount at top of page. Cut mat from flower patterned paper; tear and roll top and bottom edges; mount. Cut tan cardstock photo mat; ink edges in black and mount in offset fashion on patterned paper mat. Mat photo on white cardstock and ink edges in black. Affix fabric photo corners onto photo; wrap sheer polka-dot ribbon around right side of photo and tie. Mount piece on page. Ink edges of page in black to complete.

*Diane Enarson, Corona, California*
*Photo: Rebecca Cantu, Brownwood, Texas*

**SUPPLIES:** Patterned papers, tan textured cardstock (Chatterbox); light blue textured cardstock (Bazzill); fabric photo corners (Making Memories); transparency; black ink; white cardstock; sheer polka-dot ribbon

## Like Father, Like Son
### REVEAL A PHOTO WITH A TORN MAT

Denise created a peekaboo mat by tearing a hole to display the photo beneath. Cut section of cork for bottom border, tearing top and bottom edges; mount on black embossed paper. Print title and captions for smaller photos on transparency; heat emboss in black. Cut and attach journaling on cork with brads and attach captions onto smaller photos with spiral clips; attach two more brads on other side of cork. Mat focal photo on black cardstock; cut vellum piece same size. Tear opening to reveal photo; roll back torn edges and attach over top of photo with brads. Mount piece along with smaller photos with foam adhesive. Scan small metal charm; duplicate, enlarge and print. Cut and hang paper charms with red floss from spiral clip attached on page with brad. Affix hearts on page with foam adhesive.

*Denise Tucker, Versailles, Indiana*

**SUPPLIES:** Cork paper (Magic Scraps); black embossed paper (Books By Hand); spiral clips (WBP Hamburg); metal charm (Boutique Trims); transparency; black embossing powder; brads; foam adhesive; vellum; red floss

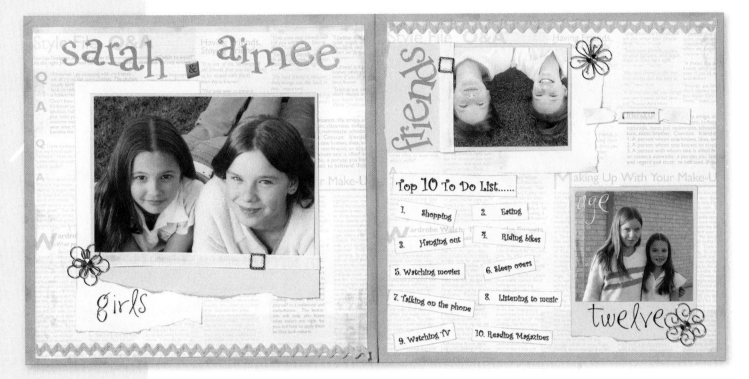

## Sarah and Aimee

### DRESS UP TORN MATS

For a touch of whimsy, Sarah added quick embellishments to her torn mats. Trim and mat two patterned papers onto two purple textured cardstock backgrounds. On left page, apply title with letter stickers and metal letter affixed on clear transparency. Mat photo on pink textured cardstock, tearing bottom edge. Ink torn edge and wrap piece with white ribbon, adding decorative buckle. Layer onto page with torn rectangle mat made from white textured cardstock, inking edges and adding rub-on word. Affix metal flower on photo corner and pink rickrack on bottom of page. On right page, mat photos on torn and inked pink textured cardstock; add words on torn sections with letter stickers and rub-on word. For upper photo, wrap with ribbon and add buckle and wire flower; mount over torn and inked white cardstock piece. Adhere remaining photo, adding wire flower. Print to-do list on white textured cardstock; cut into sections, ink edges and mount on page. Accent label holder with ribbon at each end and adhere to frame word. Affix pink rickrack across top of page.

*Sarah Moore, Banks, Canberra, Australian Capital Territory, Australia*

**SUPPLIES:** Patterned paper, wire flowers (Karen Foster Design); purple, pink and white textured cardstocks (Bazzill); letter stickers (Creative Imaginations); metal letter, rub-on words, label holder (Making Memories); buckles (Itty Bitty Buckles); clear transparency; brown ink; white ribbon; pink rickrack

## Summer Picks

### EMBELLISH MATS WITH TORN FABRIC

Melanie enhanced a denim journaling pocket by embellishing her photo mats with denim ties. Begin with two patterned paper backgrounds. On left page, affix strip cut from striped patterned paper on top of page. Mat photos on striped and polka-dot patterned papers, leaving room on focal photo mat for denim bows; mount both on page. Cut three denim strips; knot each and adhere on photo mat. Cut section from denim for pocket and stitch onto page; stamp title. Journal onto handmade paper; tear out and slip into denim pocket. Affix white rickrack along bottom of page. On right page, adhere section cut from polka-dot patterned paper on bottom and white rickrack on top of page. Mat photos on patterned paper, wrapping denim strip on bottom of focal photo mat, knotting in the middle. Mount both matted and unmatted photos on page.

*Melanie Douthit, West Monroe, Louisiana*

**SUPPLIES:** Patterned paper background, striped and polka-dot patterned papers (KI Memories); letter stamps (Stampendous!); handmade paper (Bazzill); denim strips; white rickrack

## Surf 'n Sand

### ACCENT A MAT WITH STITCHING AND TWILL TIES

Jennifer added simple stitching and tied-off twill to embellish her oversized mat. Begin with two green textured cardstock backgrounds. Journal on right side of right page. Cut strip of green patterned paper and stitch onto bottom of right page. Cut large photo mat from patterned paper; mat on white cardstock. Layer with enlarged photo matted on white cardstock. Cut photo vertically and mat along right side; machine stitch along edges of both sides of mat. Set square eyelets in upper right corner; add tied twill. Adhere larger portion of mat to left page and smaller portion to right page. Apply rub-on letters, acrylic letters and metal photo corners to photo. Crop photo and mount on right page under metal frame attached with brads. String beads and metal bird charms on fiber; attach along patterned paper strip on bottom of right page.

*Jennifer Gallacher, Savannah, Georgia*

**SUPPLIES:** Green textured cardstocks (Bazzill); patterned papers (Chatterbox, Karen Foster Design); square eyelets, metal photo corners (Making Memories); rub-on letters, metal frame (Li'l Davis Designs); metal bird charms (source unknown); twill; brads; fiber; beads

## Savor the Moments

### JOIN A MITERED CHIPBOARD FRAME WITH FABRIC STRIPS

Angelia crafted a pretty frame using fabric strips to link mitered sections of chipboard. Cut sections from plaid, flower and faux-paint patterned papers; crumple plaid section. Layer all onto faux-painted paper background. Stitch a button on each corner of crumpled paper. Mount photo on page. Cut chipboard pieces to form frame; miter and punch holes in each end. Paint pieces white; once dry, lightly sand inside edges to distress. Apply clear definition stickers to frame. Link frame together with pink fabric pieces and mount over photo. Cut out vellum quote and attach with brads. Embellish page with metal flowers attached with brads.

*Angelia Wiggington, Belmont, Mississippi*

**SUPPLIES:** Patterned papers (Chatterbox, K & Company); clear definition stickers, metal flowers (Making Memories); vellum quote (Memories Complete); buttons and pink fabric (Junkitz); chipboard pieces; white paint; fabric pieces; brads

It's nice to look back at this photo and know that this Easter is over! Jonathan was on a 4-day trip at the time, and I would have been home all alone with Talon if I didn't decide to fly down to my parents house for the holiday weekend. My sister Noel's family would be there too, with all of their kids, so I was looking forward to seeing them. I didn't know that Talon was going to be such a handful on this trip. I felt like I was running a marathon all weekend long just trying to keep up with him. Did I mention the weather was 100 degrees and we had packed sweaters and long pants. I had forgotten how hot California can get in the spring. That Sunday in church, I was really trying to enjoy my time with my family, but Talon kept on doing headstands on the pews and kicking people. He was loud, wiggly and obnoxious. Of course sitting on the pew with all of his cousins didn't help. When Talon jumped in my lap and started kicking me, I got really upset because his shoes tore a huge hole into my favorite skirt. This all happened in the first 15 minutes of the service. I took him out of the meeting out of respect to all the other people sitting around us. I chased Talon up and down the halls trying to get him to calm down. I was glad when it was finally time to go back to the house. After church, we had a nice Easter dinner prepared by my parents...that I didn't get to enjoy because Talon refused to eat anything and he just wanted to run around. I had to chase after him so he didn't break anything. My parents house is far from being "kid proof." It has always been a family tradition to take a family portrait outside. I chased Talon down so that we could pose for this photo. Looking back on this Easter portrait, I am glad that this Easter is over, but I can laugh at all of the turmoil that my dear Talon caused me. It's all trivial! He had a blast! He really enjoyed playing with his cousins, he enjoyed the hot weather and being able to play with squirt guns, he enjoyed eating candy and hunting for eggs; and in the end, thinking of all of his energy, it does put a smile on my face.

## Easter Madness

### EMBELLISH A LARGE MAT WITH STITCHED PHOTO CORNERS

Samantha dressed up her photo with stitched photo corners. Cut section of striped patterned paper; adhere on red textured cardstock background. Double mat photo on green cardstock and floral patterned paper. Cut corner pieces from green and red cardstocks; layer with light red cardstock squares. Stitch together to form two photo corners. Set eyelets in centers and mount over opposite corners on photo. Mat mini tag on red cardstock; write date, tie with wire and affix to larger photo mat. Journal on red cardstock; cut out, ink edges in red and mat on green textured cardstock. Cut thin strip from green cardstock and mount across top of page; adhere journaling. Set eyelets along right side of page. Cut letters for portion of title using stencils and green cardstock. Use actual stencil for second letter. Make into tag by setting eyelet and tying with ribbon; ink edges in green and mount all on page. Handwrite remainder of title on red cardstock; cut to fit under label holder and attach with brads.

*Samantha Walker, Battle Ground, Washington*

**SUPPLIES:** Patterned papers, stencil letters (Chatterbox); red and green textured cardstocks (Bazzill); mini tag (Stampin' Up!); label holder (Jo-Ann Fabric); red, light red and green cardstocks; eyelets; wire; red and green inks; brads

## That Was Then...

### ADD A STICKER TITLE TO OFF-CENTER MATS

By placing her photos off-center on their mats, Cheryl was able to use the extra space to apply her title. Cut patterned paper strip and adhere vertically down right side of brown textured cardstock. Double mat photos with lighter shades of brown textured cardstocks, making bottom mat larger and mounting off-center. Using foam tape, apply title using typewriter key letter stickers. Journal onto vellum; cut out, attach to patterned paper mat with brads and mount on page.

*Cheryl Kolar, Gurnee, Illinois*

**SUPPLIES:** Patterned paper (Two Busy Moms); brown textured cardstocks (Bazzill); typewriter key letter stickers (EK Success); foam adhesive; vellum; brads

# What I Remember

## EMBELLISH AN OVERSIZED MAT

Alison matted her photo off to one side and added a pre-stitched photo corner for a simple but striking look. Begin with two brown cardstock backgrounds. Cut sections of plaid, striped and circle patterned papers; mount all onto pages. For left page, cut square mat from brown circle patterned paper; mount photo printed with white border at off-set angle and adhere element to page. Cut corner from pre-stitched paper; affix over bottom right corner of mat. Sand tag, handwrite date and attach with brads. For right page, journal on pale yellow cardstock; cut out and machine stitch onto page. Cut out fabric sticker with patterned scissors and mount above journaling box.

*Alison Chabe, Charleston, Massachusetts*

**SUPPLIES:** Patterned papers (Chatterbox, Deluxe Designs); tag, pre-stitched paper, fabric sticker (Chatterbox); patterned scissors (Fiskars); brown cardstocks; brads; pale yellow cardstock

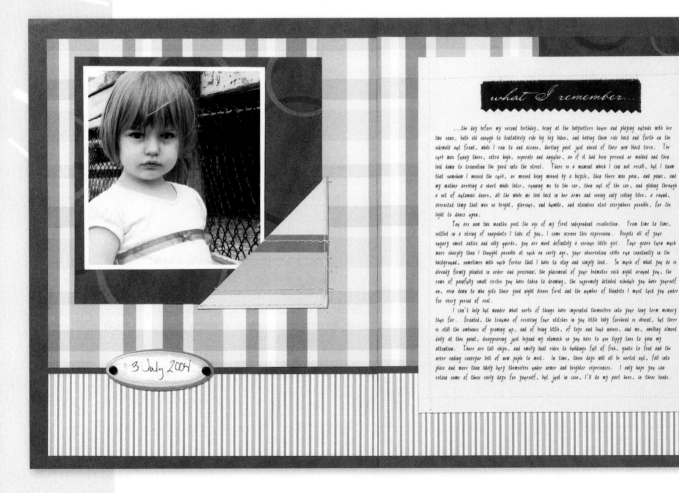

## Makayla Full of Pumpkin

### ENHANCE STACKED MATS WITH A STICKER FRAME

Michelle surrounded her little girl's photo with perfectly picked adjectives mounted on a stacked photo mat. Cut definition patterned paper and lined patterned paper into two sections; mat on rust-colored cardstock background page, adhering strip of black cardstock where papers meet. Triple mat photo on black cardstock and lined patterned paper, making bottom two mats large; cover photo with mat cut from muslin patterned paper. Affix word stickers, label stickers and labels around mat opening; mount. Use rub-on letters, label and label sticker to apply title; mount definition sticker below. Attach pumpkin charm with brad.

*Michelle Tardie, Richmond, Virginia*

**SUPPLIES:** Definition patterned paper, muslin patterned paper (Daisy D's); lined patterned paper (Chatterbox); word stickers, label stickers (Pebbles); label maker (Dymo); rub-on letters, definition sticker (Making Memories); pumpkin charm (Papyrus); brad

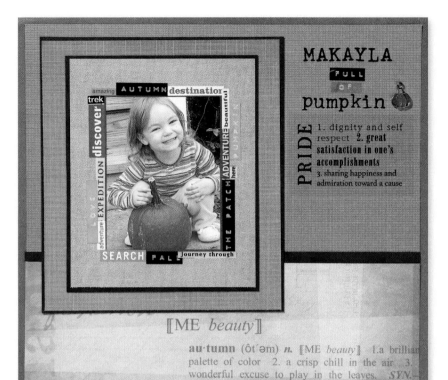

## Nature

### SWIRL A STACKED MAT

By simply stacking and rotating richly colored cardstock pieces, Linda created an appealing mat to highlight her photo. Adhere section of twill tape to bottom left corner of page; adorn with square brads and rub-on word. Cut cardstock mats from red, burgundy and orange cardstocks; layer onto page with photo. Punch circle from red cardstock to fit metal-rimmed tag; adorn with acrylic letter sticker. Wrap right side of page with ribbon, adding tag element to knot. Cover slide mount with brown cardstock; adhere over photo and then onto ribbon. Apply letter stickers for portion of title; complete with letter stamps.

*Linda Garrity, Kingston, Massachusetts*

**SUPPLIES:** Orange textured cardstock (Bazzill); square brads (Chatterbox); rub-on word (Making Memories); acrylic letter sticker, letter stickers (Creative Imaginations); slide mount (Polaroid); letter stamps (Hero Arts); brown ink; tan, red and brown cardstocks; twill; ribbon; metal-rimmed tag; circle punch

We just couldn't resist taking this precious puppy home! Sammi stole our hearts from the moment we all held her. Her sweet little face and soft fur were too tempting to pass up and we realized she needed to become part of the family.

## Puppy Love
### USE SLIDE MOUNTS TO FEATURE A PHOTO

Here a slide mount makes for a quick and easy means of framing the face of a new family companion. Mat tan cardstock on brown cardstock; layer with cut sections of patterned paper. Add leather strips mounted on brown cardstock strips to paper seams. Mount photos on cream cardstock and add to page; add slide mount. Tear one edge of journaling block; attach to page with brads. Stamp bottom left corner with letter stamps. Create title in upper right corner with stickers.

*Valerie Barton, Flowood, Mississippi*

**SUPPLIES:** Patterned paper (Design Originals); stamps (La Pluma); slide mount (Magic Scraps); stickers (Pebbles); leather strips (Offray); vellum; brads; transparency

## Sweetie
### MAT A PREMADE FRAME

Polly was able to create this layout capturing her daughter's charm by enhancing a premade mat with perfectly chosen embellishments. Begin with two coordinating patterned papers. Trim and tear bottom from one, inking torn edge in brown; mount on background. Lightly sand edges of premade frame; adhere photo beneath. Mat large sanded patterned paper mat on brown cardstock; layer onto page with framed photo. Embellish frame with silk flowers; attach buttons and decorative brad in centers. Stamp letters on twill scrap; mount on frame. Stamp journaling on inked tags and mount. Tie ribbon on bottom of page, hanging small date-stamped tag adorned with safety pin element and affix name below with letter stickers.

*Polly McMillan, Bullhead City, Arizona*

**SUPPLIES:** Coordinating patterned papers (Basic Grey); premade frame (Cropper Hopper); patterned paper mat (Creative Imaginations); decorative brad (Making Memories); die-cut letters (QuicKutz); letter stamps (PSX Design); safety pin element (Li'l Davis Designs); letter stickers (K & Company); brown and black inks; sandpaper; brown cardstock; silk flowers; buttons; twill scrap; ribbon

# CHAPTER FOUR
## *Embellishments*

## *Winter Kisses*
### PAINT METAL ACCENTS

By applying paint to her snowflake charms and metal mesh, Jennifer gave her layout a wonderful wintry feel. Cut strip of red cardstock; mount across top of black cardstock background. Paint strip of metal mesh with white acrylic paint; once dry, adhere across top of page over red strip. Cut square section of textured paper and adhere on bottom corner of page; affix red gingham ribbon along right edge. Set eyelets on bottom of enlarged photo. Paint three metal snowflakes white; affix on square metal-rimmed tags and hang from eyelets on photo. Mount photo. Punch heart from red cardstock and tuck under one metal snowflake. Journal onto transparency; cut out and attach over textured paper with eyelets. Tuck metal element under top right corner of photo; apply rub-on word for portion of title. Complete title with acrylic word. Knot ribbon and attach with colored safety pin on upper right corner of page.

*Jennifer Gallacher, Savannah, Georgia*

**SUPPLIES:** Metal mesh, metal snowflakes and square metal-rimmed tags (Making Memories); textured paper (Daisy D's); metal element, rub-on word, acrylic word, colored safety pin (Li'l Davis Designs); heart punch (Emagination Crafts); red and black cardstocks; white acrylic paint; eyelets; transparency; ribbon

So proud of her new friend, Katelyn can't resist bestowing a warm kiss on her handsome snowman. Within a few days, the weather warmed; and the snow was gone, leaving her cold companion leaning, leaning, and then falling to the ground. It was sweet how long he held on in the warming weather. He must have been reluctant to leave his sweet new friend.

## *Waiting for Her Hero, Her Daddy*
### HANG METAL CHARMS IN A BAG

Metal mesh reminiscent of a screen door and heart and key charms suspended in a tiny bag perfectly complement Amy's endearing photo. Cut metal mesh to fit white cardstock background; attach with square brads on each corner. Cut strips of patterned paper, inking edges in black. Attach one strip horizontally across bottom of page with colored brads, and one vertically on right side with colored brads. Ink paint chip and adhere on intersection of patterned paper strips. Create portion of title with labels and mount on paint chips. Apply rub-on words for remainder of title on bottom of patterned paper strip. Cut photo mat from black cardstock and attach on page with colored brad; mount photo printed with white border atop mat. Attach metal photo hanger on top of page with eyelet. Place heart, key and lock charms inside sheer bag; attach gingham ribbon to bag with decorative safety pin and secure ribbon to metal photo hanger with colored brad.

*Amy Brown, Eclectic, Alabama*

**SUPPLIES:** Square brads (Creative Impressions); patterned paper (Doodlebug Design); rub-on letters, decorative safety pin (Making Memories); metal heart hanger (source unknown); heart, key and lock charms (source unknown); metal mesh; white and black cardstocks; black ink; colored brads; sheer bag; gingham ribbon

## Tough But Tender...

### ENHANCE A MASCULINE PAGE WITH WIRE

Shelby used wire to help reflect the stronger side of her husband, then added knotted ribbon to represent his softer side. Cut section of blue patterned paper; mount on brown cardstock. Adhere thin strips cut from lined patterned paper on top and bottom of cut section. Print title and journaling on cream cardstock; cut into mat and journaling box, inking edges in brown. Mount photo on mat and adhere on page; attach journaling on photo with wire. Set pair of eyelets at top and bottom of mat; string wire through, attaching on back of page. Knot ribbons along wire. Set eyelets at page corners, stringing wire through to make borders.

*Shelby Valadez, Saugus, California*

**SUPPLIES:** Blue and lined patterned papers (Chatterbox); ribbon (Li'l Davis Designs); brown and cream cardstocks; brown ink; eyelets; wire

## Celebrate Freedom

### ADD STICKERS TO METAL-RIMMED TAGS

Photo stickers applied to metal-rimmed tags and a painted ribbon charm make a bold statement on this patriotic page. Layer a khaki cardstock background with red cardstock, star patterned paper and torn blue cardstock. Double mat photo on red and blue cardstocks; mount on right side of page. Cut photo stickers to fit metal-rimmed tags; mount all on page left of photo. Enhance ribbon charm with white acrylic paint; slide onto preprinted twill and adhere across bottom of page. Apply title on top section with rub-on words.

*Lillie Tice, Allen, Texas*
*Photo: Melodee Langworthy, Rockford, Michigan*

**SUPPLIES:** Patterned paper (source unknown); photo stickers (Pebbles); metal-rimmed tag, ribbon charm, rub-on words (Making Memories); preprinted twill (7 Gypsies); red, blue and khaki cardstocks; white acrylic paint

## Logan and Austin
### ACCENT PAPERS WITH INK

Tara used black and white inks to distress her background and give her layout an edgy feel. Ink red textured cardstock background and patterned paper section in black; mount section, leaving upper corner un-adhered to form pocket for tag. Cut tag and large section from black cardstock; ink tag in white and adorn with clock charm. Tear right edge of black cardstock section, ink in white and mount. Tuck tag into patterned paper section. Mat photo on red textured cardstock; ink in black, attach paper clip on top corner and mount. Apply title with letter stickers and rub-on word. Wrap washer-adorned gingham ribbon around bottom of page, securing on back of page. Stamp date on bottom corner of page. Stamp metal tag and tie with printed twist tie; mount. Adhere labels at top corner of page.

*Tara Daigle, Baton Rouge, Louisiana*

**SUPPLIES:** Red textured cardstock (Bazzill); patterned paper (KI Memories); clock charm (7 Gypsies); letter stickers (Creative Imaginations); rub-on word, metal tag, date stamp (Making Memories); letter stamps (PSX Design); printed twist tie (Pebbles); labels (Dymo); black and white inks; black cardstock; paper clip; gingham ribbon; washer

## Various Stages of Jake
### ADD INK DETAIL TO PAGE ELEMENTS

Lydia enhanced her papers and acrylic accents with ink for added interest. Ink edges of a white polka-dot patterned paper background in black. Cut two sections of blue polka-dot patterned paper and ink edges in black; wrap each with various ribbons and secure to backs of sections. Vertically mount each on background. Adhere focal photo. Crop remaining photos and mount side by side along bottom of page, affixing center photo with foam adhesive. Cut small squares of patterned paper to fit acrylic squares and letters. Ink edges of each; attach acrylic pieces over squares and place along top and bottom of page.

*Lydia Rueger, Memory Makers Books*

**SUPPLIES:** Patterned papers (7 Gypsies, Paper Adventures); letter stickers, acrylic squares (Creative Imaginations); acrylic letters (Li'l Davis Designs); black ink; ribbons; foam adhesive; black pen

### Little Big Man
#### ALTER ELEMENTS WITH INK

Stacey coordinated her photo mat and journaling block with a faux-inked and stamped patterned paper by inking each to match. Ink edges of photo in black; mat on white cardstock mat and ink edges. Mount on patterned paper background. Print journaling and title onto a transparency; cut both out. Mat each title on inked white cardstock and adhere.

*Stacey Stamitoles, Sylvania, Ohio*

**SUPPLIES:** Patterned paper (Scrappy Cat); black ink; white cardstock; transparency

### Just 1 More Day
#### ADD TEXTURE TO STENCILS WITH INK

Christine inked through mesh on her stencil embellishment to add rugged texture to her title. Cut strips from black cardstock and striped patterned paper; layer onto top and bottom of green textured cardstock background. Mat focal photo on white cardstock and adhere; add photo clips. Journal on transparency; cut out and mount. Crop photos and adhere on page under filmstrips. Stamp first portion of title onto transparency in white paint; stamp again with black ink to "shadow," leaving room for stencil number. Cut out and mount across top of page. Lay mesh over number stencil and ink in black; pull up mesh, mount stencil on white cardstock and adhere on title strip. Paint chipboard circles white; once dry, apply rub-on letters and affix on bottom of page. Follow with stencil number.

*Christine Brown, Hanover, Minnesota*

**SUPPLIES:** Striped patterned paper and green textured cardstock (KI Memories); photo clips, chipboard circles (7 Gypsies); filmstrips (Creative Imaginations); stencil letters, letter stamps (Ma Vinci's Reliquary); mesh (Magic Mesh); chipboard circles (Bazzill); rub-on letters (Making Memories); black ink; black and white cardstocks; transparency; black and white acrylic paint

## *Baby Delight*

### USE A PREPRINTED OVERLAY

Few embellishments are as artsy and easy as preprinted transparency overlays, and Caitlin made great use of one here. Begin with embossed patterned paper background; determine photo placement and mount. Adhere overlay on top of page, placing adhesive in areas you will cover later with journaling and embellishments. Journal on white cardstock; cut out and mat on light green cardstock. Using craft knife, cut slit in transparency so that script word will slightly overlap corner of journaling box; mount. Adhere acrylic squares on light green cardstock; trim and mount, covering adhesive beneath.

*Caitlin Luther, Selah, Washington*

**SUPPLIES:** Embossed patterned paper (K & Company); preprinted transparency overlay (Daisy D's); acrylic squares (EK Success); white and light green cardstocks

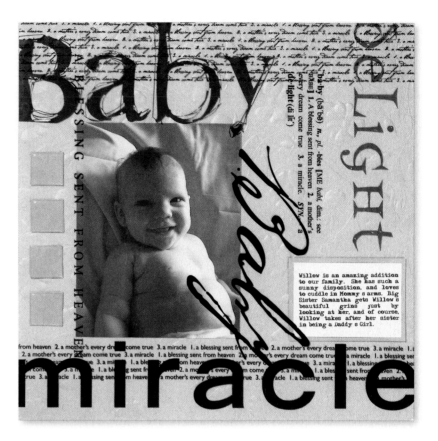

## *Grandma*

### EMBELLISH A TRANSPARENCY

MaryJo embellished a transparency with clip art to use as a backdrop for a special photo of her grandma. Using photo-editing software, create title and background for photo; print both onto transparencies and cut out. Attach pieces to white cardstock with eyelets; mount on pink cardstock background, popping title with foam adhesive. Apply text on photo; print, cut out and adhere on transparency. Embellish with lace, buttons and silk flowers.

*MaryJo Regier, Memory Makers Books*

**SUPPLIES:** Photo-editing software (Adobe); alphabet and floral clip art (Vintage Workshop); white and pink cardstocks; foam adhesive; lace; buttons; silk flowers

## Alex

### FRAME PHOTOS WITH SLIDE MOUNTS

By using printed slide mounts, Donna featured additional photos in an easy and artful way. Cut sections from printed transparency and patterned papers; layer onto green textured cardstock background, folding top right corner of patterned paper. Print photos with white border; cut and mount. Machine stitch along quadrant of top photo. Set photo turns with eyelets over bottom photo and on top of folded corner. Adhere ribbon over top photo, securing on back of page. Affix additional ribbon section over top half of page in upper left corner, embellishing with spiral clip. Crop small photos to mount beneath slide mounts. Wrap one with ribbon and mount at page corner and accent the other with spiral clip and layer over ribbon. Add date next to bottom photo with number stamps.

*Donna Leslie, Tinley Park, Illinois*

**SUPPLIES:** Printed transparency and slide mounts (Creative Imaginations); patterned papers (7 Gypsies, Colorbök, Hot Off The Press); green textured cardstock (Bazzill); photo turns (7 Gypsies); number stamps (Hero Arts); eyelets; spiral clips; ribbon

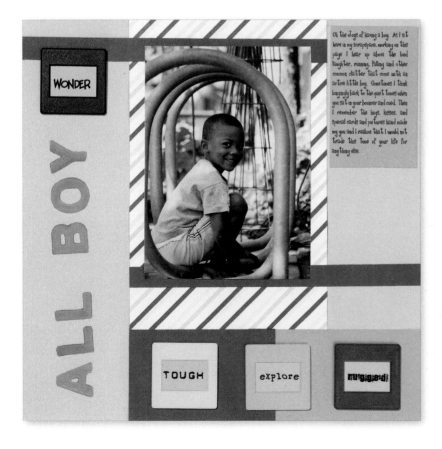

## All Boy

### SHOWCASE PREMADE SLIDE MOUNTS

Renee used preprinted slide mount embellishments to help capture the essence of her son for a quick, crisp page. Cut section of striped patterned paper; mount on tan cardstock background page. Cut sections of brown textured cardstock and blue cardstock; mount side by side on bottom of page. Cut strips of brown textured cardstock and adhere; mount photo on page atop strips. Stamp title onto right side of page using foam letter stamps and blue acrylic paint. Journal on blue cardstock; cut to size and affix. Cut desired words from premade slide mount transparencies; mat on tan cardstock and place inside slide mounts. Adhere slide mounts to page.

*Renee Hagler, Birmingham, Alabama*

**SUPPLIES:** Patterned paper, brown textured cardstock (Making Memories); foam letter stamps (Duncan); premade transparencies and slide mounts (Magic Scraps); tan and blue cardstocks; blue acrylic paint

## Friendship

### PUNCH OUT INSTANT ACCENTS

Michelle turned her page horizontally and used premade embellishments for a quick and unique page. Print journaling on an 8½ x 11" green cardstock background, rotating text accordingly. Turn page; mat photo and printed frame in offset fashion on orange cardstock and adhere. Cut section of patterned paper and affix along bottom of page. Apply title sticker and definition sticker; affix word sticker on top left corner of page. Cut strips from orange cardstock to mount under each sticker. Punch out premade flowers and adhere with foam tape.

*Michelle Tardie, Richmond, Virginia*

**SUPPLIES:** Punch-out frame and flowers (My Mind's Eye); patterned paper (Chatterbox); title, definition and word sticker (Making Memories); green and orange cardstocks; foam tape

## Junk Collector

### ALTER PREMADE ELEMENTS

Slight additions to her premade embellishments gave Jodi's quick layout a personalized look. Journal on faux-wood paneled patterned paper; cut out and mount on brown cardstock background. Add enlarged photo. Cut strips of red cardstock and adhere along top and bottom of journaling. Cut strip from ruler patterned paper and mount on top of upper cardstock strip; machine stitch at seams and on bottom strip. Adhere punch-out flowers on bottom of journaling, stitching a button between them. Die cut title from red cardstock; affix. Cut corners from premade frame; stitch one at top right corner and one on bottom right corner with strip cut from ruler paper. Stitch red button on center of large flower punch-out; mount with foam adhesive.

*Jodi Heinen, Sartell, Minnesota*

**SUPPLIES:** Patterned papers (source unknown); flower punch-outs, premade frame (My Mind's Eye); brown and red cardstocks; brown and red buttons; foam adhesive

## Celebrate
### ACCENT PUNCH-OUT SQUARES WITH EMBELLISHMENTS

Stacey used punch-outs as a base for additional embellishments. Cut sections of various patterned papers for background; ink edges in black and assemble pieces onto cardstock. Wrap photo with ribbon; mount date on back of acrylic tag and hang from ribbon. Ink paint chip, adhere to patterned paper section and mount onto page; layer with photo. Cut three square mats and circle from pink cardstock; ink edges and mount vertically down left side of page. Ink edges of patterned punch-outs and mount along with clear plastic pocket on squares. Embellish squares with page pebble, label, silk flower, metal word tags attached with brad, and vellum flower tag adorned with letter pebble and tied off with ribbon. Journal next to photo.

*Stacey Kingman, Ellsworth, Illinois*

**SUPPLIES:** Patterned papers, punch-out squares and circles (KI Memories); acrylic tag, page pebble, vellum flower tag, letter pebble (Making Memories); label (Dymo); metal word tags (Chronicle Books); clear plastic pocket (source unknown); black ink; ribbon; paint chip; pink cardstock; silk flower; brad

## All About My Son
### INCORPORATE PREMADE LABELS

Rhonda used premade punch-out labels as embellishments and to spark thoughts for her journaling. Cut section of flower patterned vellum and mount on striped patterned paper background. Mat focal photo on grid patterned paper; mount with remaining unmatted photos on page. Attach punch-out labels with brads. Set pairs of rivets on bottom right and left sides of page. Run twine through each rivet, crossing in the middle and stringing with key charm; secure twine on back of page. Cut tag from grid patterned paper; journal, tie with gingham ribbon and mount between twine pieces. Crop photo and mount beneath metal frame. Attach title punch-out threaded with twine.

*Rhonda Jones, Aloha, Oregon*

**SUPPLIES:** Flower patterned vellum, patterned papers, punch-out labels and title, rivets (Chatterbox); key charm (EK Success); metal frame (Making Memories); brads; twine

## Those Who Bring Sunshine...
### ADD FAUX DIMENSIONAL PUNCH-OUTS

A faux-stitched sun accent is a simple yet striking addition to this quick-to-create page. Print quote on white cardstock, leaving room to apply letter stickers. Add photo. Cut sections of blue textured cardstock; mount along top and bottom of page. Tear two thin strips from blue textured cardstock; mount over seams of cardstock sections and stitch to page along straight edge of each. Cut out large sun die-cut element and affix at top of page. Punch sun from remainder of paper; layer over small yellow cardstock rectangle. Stitch along edges, write date and mount. Set eyelets on either side and string with wire; join together and curl ends.

*Trish Dykes, Rathdrum, Idaho*

**SUPPLIES:** Letter stickers (SEI); blue textured cardstock (Bazzill); sun cut-out (EK Success); sun punch (Marvy); yellow cardstock; eyelets; wire

Those who
bring

to the lives
of others,
cannot
keep it from
themselves.
James Barrie

## Love That Smile!
### ADD EASY DIE-CUT ENHANCEMENTS

Janetta created a cheery layout adorned with eye-catching die cuts and punches. Cut strips from yellow textured cardstock to mount on blue textured cardstock background. Assemble 3-square die-cut border along bottom of page. Adhere die-cut photo corners onto photos printed with white border; mount on page. Mat remaining photo onto white textured cardstock. Journal on white cardstock; cut and fold into card, adhering photo inside. Mount piece cut from orange textured cardstock for card front and mount photo on top. Adhere two confetti suns together on edge of journaling card for easy opening; mount piece on page. Apply title with acrylic letters, punched sun element and exclamation die cut.

*Janetta Abucejo Wieneke, Memory Makers Books*

**SUPPLIES:** Yellow, blue, white and orange textured cardstocks (Bazzill); 3-square die cuts (QuicKutz); photo corner die cuts, exclamation point die cut (Sizzix); sun punch (EK Success); smile face punch (source unknown); acrylic letters (Heidi Grace Designs); white cardstock; confetti suns

## Bobby Pins

### INCORPORATE PRETTY RIBBON ACCENTS

Stacey incorporated a bobby pin and ribbon into her design and mused on the sentimental value they'll hold when her dancer daughters are all grown up. Print journaling on brown textured cardstock background, leaving space for additional journaling printed on pink textured cardstock. Ink edges of pink journaling in black and mount on page. Cut large section of pink textured cardstock; ink edges and mount on page. Print enlarged photo onto canvas paper; ink edges and mount. Apply title with letter stickers and photo caption with label. Set eyelets for knotted ribbons; thread various ribbons through and knot. Adorn right side of photo with metal photo corners; attach bobby pin on journaling box.

*Stacey Kingman, Ellsworth, Illinois*

**SUPPLIES:** Pink and brown textured cardstock (Bazzill); letter stickers (Doodlebug Design); label maker (Dymo); metal photo corners (Making Memories); black ink; canvas paper; eyelets; various ribbons; bobby pin

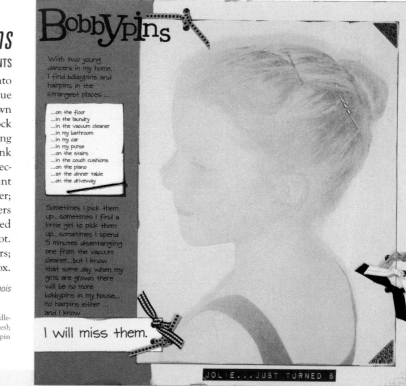

## New Jammies

### DRESS UP A PAGE WITH RIBBON ACCENTS AND TAG TOPPERS

Angelia's feminine ribbon accents create an especially pretty little-girl layout. Cut striped patterned paper section and mount on diamond patterned paper background. Affix various ribbons across bottom of page; stitch buttons onto each. Cut long photo mats from pink cardstock and flower patterned paper; mount one photo on each, using white photo corners and adhere. Accent focal photo mat with ribbon, stitched buttons and a stamped title. Flank title with patterned paper squares and brads. Embellish secondary photo mat with ribbon and stitched buttons. Stamp name onto pink cardstock and cut out; attach on ribbon with acrylic label holder and brads. Journal on white cardstock; cut into tag. Tie large button with ribbon and mount on top of tag; slide behind photo. Attach silk flower with stitched button center.

*Angelia Wiggington, Belmont, Mississippi*

**SUPPLIES:** Patterned papers (Chatterbox, K & Company, Making Memories); white photo corners (Canson); foam stamps (Making Memories); letter stamps (Rubber Stampede); label holder (KI Memories); silk flower (Michaels); plaid, polka-dot and colored ribbons (Close To My Heart, May Arts); various colored small and large buttons; pink cardstock; orange acrylic paint; black ink; colored brads

## Dream Big
### EMBELLISH A PHOTO MAT WITH RIBBONS

Here pretty ribbons provide quick and simple photo embellishments. Turn an 8½ x 11" purple cardstock background sideways. Layer with cut sections of patterned papers. Mat enlarged photo on patterned paper; tear off left edge. Wrap a twisted gingham ribbon around left side, knotting together in center. Cut sections of sheer purple polka-dot ribbon and tie each along gingham ribbon. Mount piece on page. Paint metal letters for first portion of title purple; once dry, attach with brads. Apply remainder of title with colored acrylic letter charms below photo.

*Ralonda J. Heston, Murfreesboro, Tennessee*

**SUPPLIES:** Patterned papers, colored acrylic letter charms (Doodlebug Design); metal letters (Making Memories); gingham ribbon and sheer purple polka-dot ribbon (May Arts); purple cardstock; purple paint; brads

## Autumn Walk
### TOP OFF A PAGE POCKET WITH RIBBON

Angelia used attractive decorative ribbon to conceal the seams of her paper as well as the top of the pocket that contains her journaling tag. Cut large section from patterned paper; mount on green cardstock background, forming a pocket by only adhering bottom and sides of paper. Mat focal photo on black cardstock; mount with additional photos, adding fabric photo corners on bottom corner of left photo and top corner of right photo. Attach printed ribbon across corner of focal photo with brads. Wrap wide silk ribbon around buckle, then around page at pocket opening; secure on back. Apply rub-on word onto rectangle metal-rimmed tag and hang from buckle with sheer ribbon. Punch circle from green cardstock and apply rub-on word; adhere to circle metal-rimmed tag and hang from buckle with fiber. Cut tag from green textured cardstock; cut section from patterned paper and mount on top of tag. Punch hole and tie with fiber, hanging metal flower charm. Journal on tag and slip into pocket.

*Angelia Wiggington, Belmont, Mississippi*

**SUPPLIES:** Patterned paper (Wordsworth); fabric photo corners, printed ribbon, metal flower charm (Making Memories); buckle (7 Gypsies); green textured cardstock (Bazzill); green and black cardstocks; brads; wide silk ribbon; sheer ribbon; fibers; hole punch

## Furry

### ADD BUTTONS IN AN INSTANT

Valerie incorporated self-adhesive stitched buttons for easy accents. Cut two sections of patterned paper and two strips of blue textured cardstock to mount on two green textured cardstock background pages; adhere patterned paper sections on bottom and cardstock strips on top of both backgrounds. On left page, mat desired photos on white cardstock and crop others; mount all photos on page. String beads onto wire, curling ends when word is formed; mount on corresponding photo. String "xoxo" on spiral clip and attach onto bottom corner of another photo. Apply title with letter stickers. Embellish page with stitched buttons. On right page, mat desired photos on white cardstock. Journal on vellum, cut out and mount on page along with photos. String letter beads on wire and on spiral clip; attach on photos. Embellish page with stitched buttons.

*Valerie Barton, Flowood, Mississippi*

**SUPPLIES:** Patterned papers (Scrap Ease); blue and green textured cardstocks (Bazzill); letter beads (Darice); letter stickers (Creative Imaginations); white cardstock; wire; spiral clips; stitched buttons; vellum

The kids were so mesmerized by these furry little creatures. They begged Daddy to let them keep them as pets, but he didn't go for it. Our compromise was to have a photo shoot with the bunnies, so they could always remember them. Even though we only had them for one afternoon, they each named their favorite. I hope Marshmellow and Oreo enjoyed their time as part of the family. We sure did!

Things that make Quinn happy... **S**winging high... **D**ressing up... **I**ce cream... **D**umbo... 'Princess' dresses... **P**icking flowers... **M**ud... **S**and... **K**nock-knock jokes... **T**he colour yellow... **D**ora The Explorer... **I**ndoor picnics... **B**ugs... **T**he park... **M**ummy-Baby time... **H**ugs... **P**inecones... **H**er friend, Robert... **H**er sister, Katja... **C**hocolate milk... **B**eing **O**utside... **A**nimals, real and toy... **F**ruit and Veggies... **2002**

## Happy Go Lucky Girl

### ADD EASY-TO-MAKE FABRIC FLOWERS

LauraLinda re-created the flowers from her little girl's dress with fabric, rickrack and buttons. Begin with two blue patterned paper backgrounds. Cut large section from blue cardstock and machine stitch onto left page; run stitch along edges of right page. Cut section from red cardstock; adhere photos and mount vertically. Cut three lengths of green rickrack for flower stems; machine stitch. Cut three 3½" circles from red fabric. Turn edge, gather and stitch. Tie off, stitch buttons onto centers and mount onto stems. Stamp title on white cardstock, cut into strips and attach with staples. For right page, mat all photos on red cardstock; adhere together onto page, placing focal photo on top and center of other photos. Journal on white cardstock; cut out and mount on bottom of page. Accent with machine-stitched red rickrack.

*LauraLinda Rudy, Markham, Ontario, Canada*

**SUPPLIES:** Blue patterned papers (Bo-Bunny Press); letter stamps (PSX Design); red fabric (Robin's Nest); blue, red and white cardstocks; green and red rickrack; staples

## Treasured Memories

### ADD ELEMENTS FROM OLD CLOTHING

For a fun embellishment inspired by her photo, Deanna incorporated the buckle from her son's old overalls. Dry brush pale yellow acrylic paint onto a light blue textured cardstock background. Affix blue coastal netting across top half of page. Adhere cut denim overall strap on upper right corner. Quadruple mat photos on pale yellow and light blue cardstocks and dark blue textured cardstock; fold upper left corner of mats over. Adhere button threaded with fiber to folded corner. Adhere remaining photo. Print title onto rectangle vellum metal-rimmed tags. Set eyelets in tags and string with bead chain; adhere over netting. Journal on blue textured cardstock; cut out, mat on dark blue textured cardstock, and mount on page with foam adhesive. Embellish corner with metal photo corner.

*Deanna Hutchison, Langley, British Columbia, Canada*

**SUPPLIES:** Light and dark blue textured cardstocks (Bazzill); metal photo corner and rectangle and metal-rimmed tags (Making Memories); blue coastal netting (Magic Scraps); denim overall strap; fiber; button; pale yellow acrylic paint; white and light blue cardstocks; eyelets; bead chain; foam adhesive

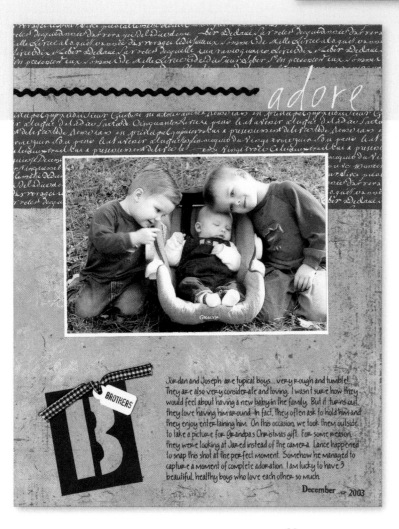

## Adore

### TRIM A PAGE WITH RICKRACK

A simple addition of rickrack provided the perfect trim for this page. Journal onto bottom right corner of distressed patterned paper background. Cut section of script-patterned paper and mount on top of page. Layer with strip of distressed patterned paper. Apply title with rub-on word. Affix rickrack across strip. Mat photo on white cardstock and mount. Using letter stencil, trace letter onto distressed patterned paper; cut out and mat on black cardstock. Adhere alongside journaling. Tie small printed tag with ribbon and affix on top of stencil letter piece. Stamp date on bottom right corner of page.

*Jennifer Miller, Humble, Texas*

**SUPPLIES:** Patterned papers (7 Gypsies, Patchwork Paper Design); rub-on word, date stamp, "brothers" tag (Making Memories); rickrack (Wrights); white and black cardstocks; letter stencil

## Beautiful

Mackenzie,

I love these pictures of you and Camryn. They are my favorites. You are such a beautiful girl. Your sweet spirit is especially lovely to me. I am inspired by your cheerful attitude and zeal for life. Thank you for teaching me about true beauty.

I Love You,
Mom

## Beautiful

### INCORPORATE RICKRACK BORDERS

Kelly added rickrack borders to her understated page design. Begin with two white cardstock backgrounds. Journal on right side of 12 x 12" lavender textured cardstock; tear below journaling as well as bottom third of page. Add rickrack and mount sections on pages. On left page, mat enlarged photo on black textured cardstock; tear bottom of mat. Wrap with sheer ribbon, add metal heart and mount. Apply title with letter stickers. On right page, mat photos on black textured cardstock. Tear edge of one mat and mount all on page. Cut lavender textured cardstock to fit beneath slide mounts. Tie slide mounts with sheer ribbons adorned with metal letter charms; adhere on page over cardstock pieces. Add date with number stickers.

*Kelly Lee, Lake Forest Park, Washington*

**SUPPLIES:** Lavender and black textured cardstocks (Bazzill); metal heart charm (Jo-Ann Fabric); metal letter charms (Making Memories); letter and number stickers (EK Success); black rickrack; sheer ribbon

2001

## Everyday Precious Moments

### ADD TITLE WORDS TO TAGS

Here tags double as endearing page accents and as mats for a title. Cut section of striped patterned paper; tear top edge and mount on pink textured cardstock background. Journal on vellum; tear out and attach with mini eyelets. Print photo with white border and ink edges in green. Mat photo onto light green linen paper; ink edges in green. Cut section from floral patterned paper; tear off bottom edge and ink torn edge in green. Layer with matted photo and mount. Using tag template, cut tags from light green linen paper and ink edges in green. Embellish with flowers from patterned paper. Print title on vellum; tear each word out and attach on tags with mini brads. Tie tags with green gingham ribbon and mount on page.

*Sandra Liddell, Stansbury Park, Utah*

**SUPPLIES:** Patterned papers (Chatterbox); pink textured cardstock (Bazzill); mini eyelets (Darice); tag template (Provo Craft); vellum; green ink; green gingham ribbon

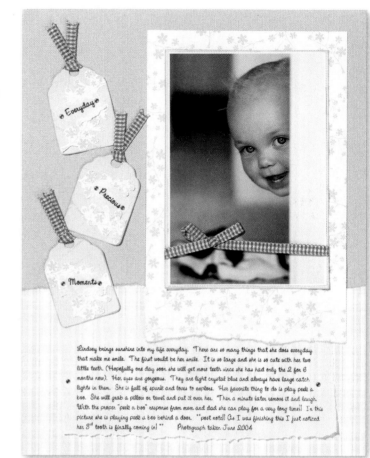

## Daughters

### INCORPORATE PRE-EMBELLISHED TAGS

Diane achieved the look of decorated tags without all the trouble by using premade tag cut-outs. Cut section of striped patterned paper; ink edges and affix vertically along left side of green cardstock background. Cut section of printed paper; lightly crumple, ink edges and mount along bottom of page. Mat photo on white cardstock. Cut second mat from plaid patterned paper; ink edges and mat again on brown textured cardstock. Layer photo and mats onto page. Journal on white cardstock; cut, ink edges and mount on page. Wrap charm-adorned ribbon around bottom of page, securing on back. Cut out large and small tag accents. Tie large tag with ribbon and adhere with foam adhesive; mount smaller tag over ribbon with foam adhesive.

*Diane Enarson, Corona, California*
*Photo: Kiddie Kandid/Babies R Us*

**SUPPLIES:** Patterned papers (Daisy D's); brown textured cardstock (Bazzill); ribbon charm (Making Memories); tag cut-outs (My Mind's Eye); black ink; ribbon (May Arts); green and white cardstocks; foam adhesive

## Dino View
### CREATE CLAY TAG EMBELLISHMENTS

With the use of clay and the foot of her son's toy dinosaur, Sheila was able to create clay elements reminiscent of fossils. Adhere focal photo on a patterned paper background. Cut rectangle and square sections to flank photo from green textured cardstock; ink edges in black, accent with cream-colored paint and mount. Stamp portion of title on rectangle with foam letter stamps and paint. Complete title with rub-on word. Adhere photo on upper right corner of page. Journal on cream-colored textured cardstock; cut out, ink in brown, handwrite date and adhere on green cardstock square. Set eyelets in twill tape; wrap twill across top of page, securing on back. Cut squares for cropped photos from green textured cardstock; ink edges, adhere photos, punch holes and hang from eyelets with twine. For clay tags, roll out paper clay to 1/8" thickness; cut three small circles, stamp with dinosaur footprint and punch holes in two of the tags. Bake according to directions, then chalk. Hang two clay tags from twill with twine; mount other clay piece over journaling.

*Sheila Doherty, Couer D'Alene, Idaho*

**SUPPLIES:** Patterned paper (Basic Grey); green and white textured cardstocks (Bazzill); foam letter stamps, rub-on word (Making Memories); paper clay (Creative Paperclay Company); twill tape (Creek Bank Creations); black and brown inks; paint; eyelets; black and tan twine; chalk; hole punch; dinosaur toy

---

We've taken many visits to the San Diego Wild Animal Park, but I don't think you ever got so excited over anything as you did seeing the Dino Mountain exhibit. We walked through the exhibit three times our first time there. When we got home you told Daddy we saw "di-osaurs n el-phants" (they had a new baby elephant there as well). So for the next weeks each day you asked if we were going to see the dinosaurs and elephants that day. I did take you several more times before the exhibit closed and you were always excited to see them. Especially the spitting dinosaur that would spray you with water. Or the baby dinosaurs just hatching from their eggs. I loved seeing the joy of discovery on your face. 6/04

---

## Jump Into Fall
### STAMP A TAG TITLE

Tricia used letter stamps applied to tags for an easy and appealing title treatment. Cut sections of various patterned papers and layer onto faux wood-patterned paper. For photo corners and journaling tab, ink three tags with walnut ink. Set one aside and wrap two around top left and bottom right corners of photo; attach with brads. Adhere photo. Journal on patterned paper; cut out using decorative edges scissors along bottom edge. Attach remaining inked tag with brad and mount on right side of page. Ink small and large tags with walnut ink; once dry, stamp with large and small letter stamps. Tie with fiber and mount.

*Tricia Rubens, Castle Rock, Colorado*

**SUPPLIES:** Patterned papers, walnut ink (Rusty Pickle); patterned scissors (Provo Craft); large letter stamps (River City Rubber Works); small letter stamps (Wal-Mart); various tags; brads; fibers

When we rake leaves for the first time in fall, our work is done halfhearted. The kids always jump in and mess any pile we have created, which means we will have to do the raking all over again. Actually we will jump right in with them. What fun! You are never too old to jump in the fall leaves!

## You Are My Girl
### EMBELLISH WITH LETTER STICKERS

Heather accented her black-and-white photo with colorful letter stickers. Ink edges of white cardstock background in black; turn page 90 degrees. Affix colored molding strips horizontally across page. Wrap and tie bottom of photo with black gingham ribbon. Cut mat from patterned paper; adhere photo at askew angle onto page with mat. Apply various letter stickers to each molding strip; attach brads on top strip. Create label for title; affix on bottom strip.

*Heather Preckel, Swannanoa, North Carolina*

**SUPPLIES:** Patterned paper, colored molding strips, letter stickers (Chatterbox); label maker (Dymo); white cardstock; black ink; brads

## Life's Little Expressions
### ADD LAYERED STICKER ACCENTS

Sharon created dimension in no time by layering stickers. Print title onto tangerine-colored textured cardstock background. Print journaling and horizontal mat for series of photos onto lime-colored textured cardstock; mat both on black cardstock and affix to top and bottom of page. Adhere series of overlapped black-and-white photos onto upper section and color photo on bottom section. Embellish page with dimensional flower stickers as desired and square brads at bottom corner.

*Sharon Whitehead, Vernon, British Columbia, Canada*

**SUPPLIES:** Tangerine and lime-colored textured cardstocks (Bazzill); dimensional flower stickers (K & Company); square brads (Making Memories); black cardstock

**WHO COULD RESIST THAT FACE!**
You make a face, I giggle, you make another face, I laugh, you giggle, I take a picture, you make a face...and so it goes. I delight in every moment that I get to spend with you. Best of all I love those 'kisses for Nana'.          June/2004

## Kemah Boardwalk

### COMBINE A VARIETY OF STICKERS

A variety of stickers made for easy enhancements for Julie's page. Cut two mats from patterned paper; round select corners and mount on opposite corners of blue cardstock background. Adhere photo on the left side of the upper mat. Attach stickers next to photo with brads. Journal on white textured cardstock; cut out and punch several small holes along top. Enhance edge with pink ink, add sticker on bottom, tie with various ribbons and mount. On lower mat, affix title on bottom with letter stickers and brads; embellish with additional stickers. Mount remaining photo and stickers along bottom left corner of page. Attach ribbon across center of page to finish.

*Julie Johnson, Seabrook, Texas*

**SUPPLIES:** Patterned paper, stickers (Karen Foster Design); white textured cardstock (Bazzill); blue cardstock; corner rounder; brads; pink ink; ribbons

## Fearless

### INCORPORATE DIMENSIONAL STICKERS

Dimensional stickers provided a quick and simple solution for adding playful touches to Janetta's page. Cut two strips from purple textured cardstock; mount vertically on left side of yellow textured cardstock background. Cut section of green textured cardstock and mount along bottom of page. Adhere cropped photos down left side of page. Double mat focal photo on green and purple textured cardstocks; mount. Stamp initials and date on purple textured cardstock; cut into square and mount below focal photo. Punch letters for title from alphabet patterned paper and mount down center of page. Journal on vellum; cut out and affix on bottom of page. Mount dimensional stickers.

*Janetta Abucejo Wieneke, Memory Makers Books*
*Photos: Jason Paluda, Westminster, Colorado*

**SUPPLIES:** Purple textured cardstock (DieCuts with a View); green and yellow textured cardstocks (Bazzill); letter and date stamps (Close To My Heart); alphabet-patterned paper (American Crafts); dimensional stickers (Sandylion, Westrim); circle punch (EK Success)

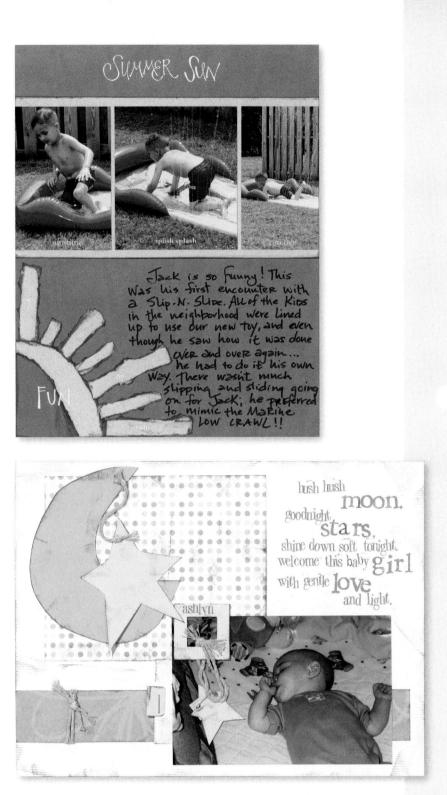

## Summer Sun

### PAPER PIECE A PAGE ELEMENT

Vanessa used torn pieces of cardstock to fashion a quick and unique embellishment for her fun summer page. Cut section from yellow speckled cardstock, ink edges in black and mount across top of blue cardstock background. Adhere photos. Apply rub-on words onto photos and on top of page for title. Tear pieces of yellow speckled cardstock for sun element; ink edges and piece together onto bottom left corner of page. Embellish with rub-on words. Journal with black pen.

*Vanessa Spady, Virginia Beach, Virginia*

**SUPPLIES:** Yellow speckled cardstock (Club Scrap); rub-on words (Making Memories); black ink; blue cardstock; black pen

## Hush Hush Moon

### HANDCUT CREATIVE ACCENTS

With a precious picture of her sleeping daughter for inspiration, Tania pieced together charming stars and a paper moon. Turn 8½ x 11" white textured cardstock sideways; ink in brown. Cut orange patterned paper strip; ink in brown and adhere across bottom of page, tying fiber around left side. Cut section of polka-dot patterned paper, ink edges and mount. Affix photo, leaving center un-adhered to accommodate journaling tag. Journal on white cardstock and cut into tag. Create pull-tab from blue cardstock and staple to tag; ink in brown and slip behind photo. Stamp lullaby on background using letter stamps. Handcut large and small stars and moon from yellow and blue cardstocks; ink in brown. Hang larger star from moon with fiber and mount together. Ink paper slide mount; stamp name with letter stamps. Adorn smaller star with safety pin and hang from slide mount with fiber; adhere over photo.

*Tania Willis, Columbus, Ohio*

**SUPPLIES:** White textured cardstock (Hollo's Paper Supply); patterned papers (KI Memories); letter stamps (Hero Arts, Making Memories); brown ink; fiber; white, blue and yellow cardstocks; staple; safety pin

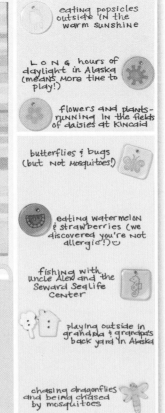

eating popsicles outside in the warm sunshine

L O N G hours of daylight in Alaska (means more time to play!)

flowers and plants- running in the fields of daisies at Kincaid

butterflies & bugs (but not mosquitoes!)

eating watermelon & strawberries (we discovered you're not allergic!)

fishing with Uncle Alex and the Seward Sealife Center

playing outside in grandma & grandpa's back yard in Alaska

chasing dragonflies and being chased by mosquitoes

just a few of Danny's favorites from summer 2003 · Anchorage, Alaska

## Summer Lovin'
### ADD ACRYLIC ACCENTS

Acrylic baubles were cleverly used to reflect the content of Anna's journaling. Cut extra large mat from plaid patterned paper and mount on color-blocked patterned paper background; adhere photo. Apply title with letter stickers. Write partial journaling below title. Journal down right side of page, adding appropriate acrylic baubles.

*Anna Armendariz, McChord Air Force Base, Washington*

**SUPPLIES:** Patterned paper (Daisy D's); color-blocked patterned paper (My Mind's Eye); letter stickers (Karen Foster Design, KI Memories); acrylic baubles (Doodlebug Design)

## Cute Ears
### ENHANCE JOURNALING WITH ACRYLIC BAUBLES

Placing acrylic baubles over select words in her journaling was a great way for MaryAnn to add visual interest. For the background, layer faux-paint patterned paper with cut sections and strips of white cardstock and grass patterned paper. Mat grass strip on cardstock strip and mount vertically along right side of background. Stitch on selected pieces. Journal on white cardstock; cut out, mat on blue cardstock, and affix small rectangle baubles onto desired words. Wrap box with ribbon and adorn with acrylic ribbon charm. Hang letter charm from jump ring off of ribbon; mount piece on page. Affix ribbon across center of page. Double mat photo on white and blue cardstocks; apply name onto photo with rub-on letters and mount on page. Apply title onto acrylic tag with rub-on words; back tag with patterned paper, tie off with ribbon and adhere.

*MaryAnn Wise, The Woodlands, Texas*

**SUPPLIES:** Grass-patterned paper (Colorbök); faux-paint patterned paper (Carolee's Creations); small rectangle baubles, word rub-ons (Making Memories); acrylic ribbon charm, acrylic tag (Creek Bank Creations); letter charm (QuicKutz); white and blue cardstocks; ribbons; jump ring

BERRILL

cute ears

Berrill went with her Brownie troop to see "The Elves & the Shoemaker" at a children's theater outside of Houston. In the play there were three little girls who were playing the elves and they were so adorable. They had pointy elf ears! Berrill was entranced! On the way home she asked me if we had any Band Aides at home. I knew she was up to something. When we got home she immediately made her own elf's ears out of Bandaides! For the next three days, my Berrill was an elf. She even wore them to school. She didn't care what the other kids said. In her mind, she was an Elf! Our neighbor, Mary Ann, had to take a picture, it was so cute and funny. I asked Mrs. Stanley, her first grade teacher if she noticed and she at first thought Berrill had surgery or some procedure on her ears, so she didn't want to say anything. Then she laughed when I told her the story. I wonder if Berrill will remember wearing Elf's ears to school.

## Cola Queen

### INCORPORATE EPHEMERA

Ginger used Coca-Cola playing cards for fun tags and additions. Begin with two blue patterned paper backgrounds. Cut strips of red cardstock; mount on bottom of left page and top of right page. For left page, double mat photo on white and blue cardstocks. Print date on blue cardstock; cut and mount on bottom of mat. Add page pebbles. Cut tag from white cardstock; layer with cropped playing cards. Print title onto white cardstock; tear out and chalk in red and blue. Attach title on tag; punch hole in tag. Cut playing card element to adhere under label holder; add eyelets. Tie tag with fibers, hanging label holder and mount. Cut remaining photos and additional playing cards into squares and adhere. Cut card to fit metal frames and add to page. For right page, repeat focal photo mat and tag techniques; add torn and chalked card to tag. Mat secondary photo on red cardstock and mount. Journal on white cardstock, tear and chalk in red and blue; affix on page. Cut remaining photos and cards into squares; mount along bottom of journaling box.

*Ginger McSwain, Cary, North Carolina*

**SUPPLIES:** Patterned papers (source unknown); page pebbles, label holders, metal frames (Making Memories); red, white and blue cardstocks; red and blue chalks; Coca-Cola playing cards; red and blue eyelets; fibers

## Nature vs. Nurture
### FEATURE RETRO PAGE ELEMENTS

Shelley added vintage images and vibrant fabrics to this page dedicated to notions of femininity. Ink edges of cream textured cardstock background in brown. Stamp title using letter stamps and multicolored ink pad. Mount section of black cardstock across center of page. Layer with cut section of patterned fabric, rounding corners. Ink edges of photo and affix. Mount denim strip across mat; adorn with colored spiral clips and knotted ribbons. Cover small photos with film negative overlays and attach to spiral clips. Journal on patterned paper; cut out and mount. Cut mats from pink and purple fabric papers; round corners and mount on page, adhering photo. Create tag from patterned paper; mount on page with small photo, adorning with square buttons. Embellish bottom left corner of page by attaching colored square conchos over number sticker matted on black cardstock and letter stickers affixed on patterned paper. Add letter stickers on number square. Stamp date on bottom of page.

*Shelley Rankin, Fredericton, New Brunswick, Canada*

**SUPPLIES:** Cream textured cardstock (Bazzill); letter stamps (Fontwerks); colored spiral clips and colored square conchos (Scrapworks); film negative overlays (Creative Imaginations); patterned paper for tag (Basic Grey); square buttons (Making Memories); patterned paper for journaling (Daisy D's); number sticker, letter stickers (Karen Foster Design); date stamp (Avery); pink and purple fabric papers (Michael Miller Memories); brown ink; multicolored ink pad; black cardstock; patterned fabric; corner rounder; denim trim; ribbons

## Mommy, Come Play With Me!
### INCLUDE MEMORABILIA ACCENTS

Here vintage playing cards perfectly supplement Kimberly's playtime layout. Print title and journaling on an orange cardstock background. Cut section of polka-dot patterned paper and mount across center of page. Border with two strips of striped patterned paper. Mat photo on white cardstock with black photo corners; mount on page. Mat vintage playing cards in offset fashion on red and blue cardstock and pink textured cardstock mats. Punch holes at top of each and tie with pink, blue and yellow gingham ribbons; adhere along bottom of page. Write date on cream-colored cardstock; cut to fit silver oval frame; mount.

*Kimberly Kesti, Phoenix, Arizona*

**SUPPLIES:** Patterned papers (Scrapworks, SEI); black photo corners (Canson); pink textured cardstock (Bazzill); silver oval frame (Nunn Design); orange, white, red and blue cardstocks; vintage playing cards; pink, blue and yellow gingham ribbons

## Serene Happiness
### ADD MICA FOR AN EARTHY FEEL

Deanna artistically enhanced her title with mica. Begin with a patterned paper background. Sand edges of photo, add photo corners altered with metallic rub-ons and mat on orange and brown cardstocks, leaving room for embellishments; ink edges in brown. Cut square from dark rust cardstock; layer with matted photo. Apply letter stickers to photo with foam adhesive and add decorative square brads to mat. Print title on fabric strip and wrap diagonally across page; secure on back. Layer with mica tiles applied with dimensional adhesive. Ink envelope in brown and mount. Punch hole in envelope flap and tie with twine; wrap around left side of layout and secure on back of page. Embellish envelope with patterned paper scrap, T-pin, skeleton and fern leaves. Print "Bliss" on fabric strip and affix on envelope. Snip ends off square brads and affix on mica tiles; add to collage. Tear bottom edges of definition stickers and ink in brown; mat on dark rust cardstock strips, tearing off bottom edge of mats. Adhere vertically on page with foam adhesive. Tie ends together with twine.

*Deanna Hutchison, Langley, British Columbia, Canada*

**SUPPLIES:** Black photo corners (Canson); metallic rub-ons (Craf-T); letter stickers, T-pin, (EK Success); square decorative brads, definition stickers (Making Memories); mica (USArtQuest); dimensional adhesive (JudiKins); orange, brown and dark rust-colored cardstocks; envelope; brown ink; foam adhesive; skeleton and fern leaves

## The Dunk
### ENHANCE AN OUTDOORS PAGE WITH ORGANICS

Here MaryJo perfectly embellished an outdoor layout with earthy accents, including mica and skeleton leaves. Trim and mat brown patterned paper on tree patterned paper. Using image-editing software, crop photos and place around enlarged focal photo; print with white border and mat on green patterned paper. Mount on page, leaving room for leaf embellishments. Apply title with leather letters. Journal on white cardstock; cut to fit leather label holder. Adorn with mica chips and mount on page. Cut tag from green patterned paper; print tag caption on white cardstock, cut out and adhere over skeleton leaf. Mount on right side of page with remaining leaves. Add stitched twine on tag and enclose small feather.

*MaryJo Regier, Memory Makers Books*

**SUPPLIES:** Brown, green and tree patterned papers (Hot Off The Press); image-editing software (ArcSoft); leather letters (EK Success); leather label holder (Making Memories); mica chips (USArtQuest); white cardstock; skeleton leaves; twine; feathers

The view from the bridge over the Dunn's River Falls at the Ruins Plantation. *Breathtaking!*

The Jungle at the *Ruins* A Jamaican Plantation

## The Jungle at the Ruins
### FASHION A PAPER CLAY EMBELLISHMENT

Here lush nature photos were complemented with an eye-catching organic embellishment. Trim ½" from left side of green textured cardstock background; ink edge in brown. Cut, ink and layer strips from sienna and dark green textured cardstock, affixing along back of trimmed edge. Mat photos on orange textured cardstock; ink edges and adhere. Handwrite date next to small photo. Print journaling and part of title on light green textured cardstock; cut and tear off bottom edge. Ink edges, wrap with fibers, gathering in center; mount skeleton leaves. Adhere title and journaling box on page. Using computer font as guide, cut remaining title with a craft knife from sienna cardstock; ink lightly and mount. Attach decorative brad on bottom corner. Roll paper clay to a ¼" thick disc; press compass stamp into clay and let dry overnight. Paint disc. When dry, ink edges and apply watermark ink to top. Sprinkle with pigment powders. Affix over gathered fibers.

*Pamela James, Ventura, California*

**SUPPLIES:** Green, dark green, light green, sienna and orange textured cardstocks (Bazzill); decorative brad (EK Success); paper clay (Creative Paperclay Company); compass stamp (Stampabilities); pigment powder (LuminArte); watermark ink (Tsukineko); brown ink; fibers; skeleton leaves; craft knife; paint

## Beautiful
### ADD A WOOD EMBELLISHMENT

Shannon's scrap piece of bead board made for an excellent journaling block and at the same time enhanced her large wooden letter accent. Cut two strips from polka-dot patterned paper and mount on top and bottom of red patterned paper background. Mat photos on tan cardstock and mount on page. Enhance wood letter with brown chalk, stamp title with letter stamps and red ink and affix on page. Print journaling onto transparency; cut out and adhere on scrap piece of wood. Wrap with ribbon, tie and mount on page.

*Shannon Taylor, Bristol, Tennessee*

**SUPPLIES:** Polka-dot and red patterned papers (Rusty Pickle); wood letter (Darice); letter stamps (Hero Arts); brown chalk; red ink; transparency; scrap wood piece; ribbon

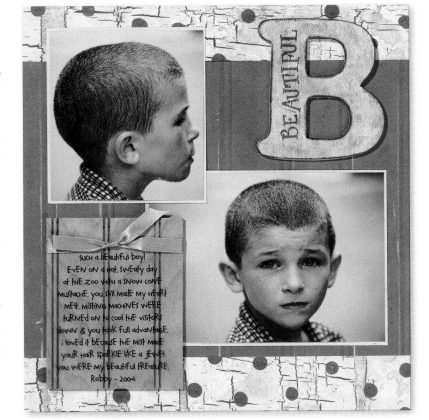

BEAUTIFUL B

SUCH a beautiful boy! Even on a hot, sweaty day at the Zoo with a snow cone mustache, you still made my heart melt. Misting machines were turned on to cool the visitors down & you took full advantage. I loved it because the mist made your hair sparkle like a jewel. you were my beautiful treasure. Robby - 2004

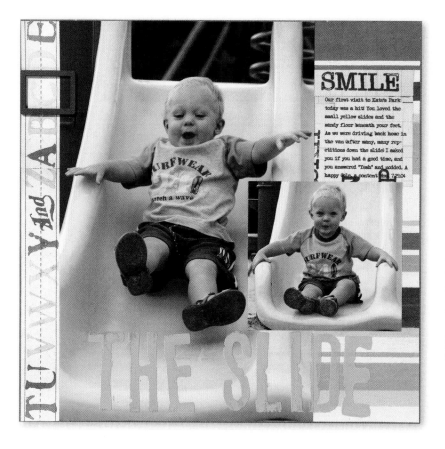

## The Slide

**PAINT AN ELEMENT TO MATCH YOUR PAGE**

With a little paint, Joanna altered the wood frame placed over the first letter of her son's name to perfectly match her layout. Cut sections of striped and alphabet patterned papers; mount on red patterned paper background. Adhere enlarged photo onto background. Using foam stamps and blue paint, stamp title on bottom of photo. Journal on notebook patterned paper; cut and mount. Adhere cropped photo. Paint wood frame red; once dry, mount over desired letter on alphabet paper.

*Joanna Bolick, Fletcher, North Carolina*

**SUPPLIES:** Patterned papers (Li'l Davis Designs, Rusty Pickle); wood frame (Li'l Davis Designs); foam letter stamps (Making Memories); blue and red paint

## Tall Stacks

**HIGHLIGHT SLIDE MOUNTS WITH PAINT**

Barb used vibrant paint to enhance her slide mount embellishments. Cut strip of red cardstock and mount vertically on left side of patterned paper background. Double mat focal photo on white textured cardstock and green cardstock. Double mat smaller photo, using white textured cardstock and red cardstock. Mount all photos. Journal on transparency; cut out and highlight desired words by applying white paint on back of transparency; mount on page. Stamp title using foam letter stamps and acrylic paint. Paint slide mounts; once dry, mount on page with foam adhesive over date sticker and photo. Add souvenir accent to finish.

*Barb Hogan, Cincinnati, Ohio*

**SUPPLIES:** Striped patterned paper (SEI); foam letter stamps (Making Memories); slide mounts (Boxer Scrapbook Productions); blue, red and green cardstocks; acrylic paint

## Christmas 2003
### ADD SPARKLE WITH JEWEL ACCENTS

Susan easily added an element of whimsy to her holiday page with a scattering of brightly colored acrylic jewels. Print title onto a white cardstock background. Layer with red cardstock that has been torn along the bottom to reveal title. Stamp Christmas tree; cut star from white cardstock and adhere. Mat one photo on crumpled white cardstock; mount others onto page and stamp photo captions for each. Attach metal snowflake with brad. Adhere acrylic jewels along stamped image and title.

*Susan Cyrus, Broken Arrow, Oklahoma*

**SUPPLIES:** Christmas tree stamp (Wordsworth); letter stamps (All Night Media, Hero Arts); acrylic jewels (Me & My Big Ideas); eyelet charm and brad (Making Memories); white cardstock; black ink

## Splash Down
### DANGLE BAUBLES FROM AN OVERSIZED PIN

MaryJo easily added an element of fun by dangling baubles from a safety pin, which nicely complement her acrylic title letters. Print focal photo with white border; mount on blue and purple patterned paper background. Journal on polka-dot patterned paper; cut out, mat off-set on yellow cardstock and mount. Mat remaining photos on yellow and white cardstocks and adhere all to page. Apply title with acrylic letters; add sun element. Attach charms on pin and adhere to page.

*MaryJo Regier, Memory Makers Books*

**SUPPLIES:** Blue and polka-dot patterned papers, acrylic letters and sun (Heidi Grace Designs); charms, pin (Blue Moon Beads); white and yellow cardstocks

# CHAPTER FIVE
## *journaling*

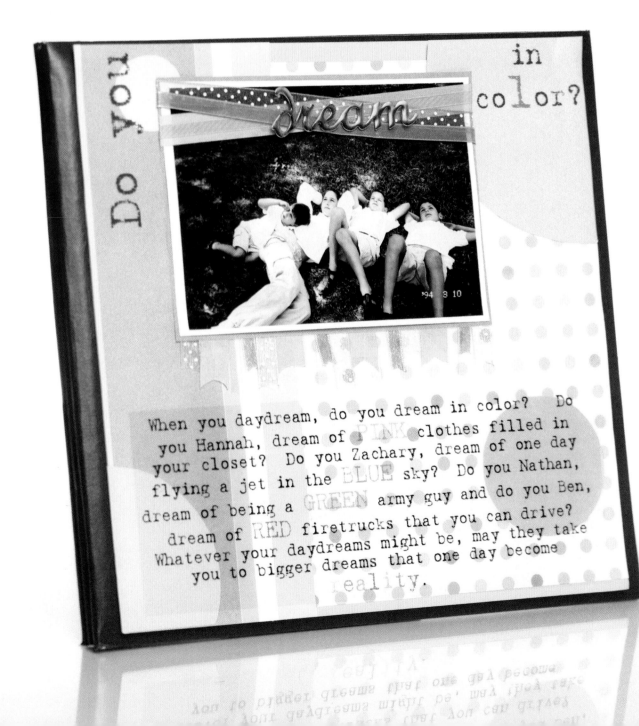

Do you *dream* in color?

When you daydream, do you dream in color? Do you Hannah, dream of PINK clothes filled in your closet? Do you Zachary, dream of one day flying a jet in the BLUE sky? Do you Nathan, dream of being a GREEN army guy and do you Ben, dream of RED firetrucks that you can drive? Whatever your daydreams might be, may they take you to bigger dreams that one day become reality.

## Exit the Past
### COMBINE STAMPED, PRINTED AND RUB-ON FONTS

Here beautiful poetic journaling is given artful drama with a combination of stamped, printed and rub-on fonts. Cut sections of striped and circle patterned papers; mount on lavender linen cardstock background. Affix molding strips along top and bottom edges of patterned papers. Stamp initial in lavender ink and caption in black ink on tag with letter stamps. Wrap bottom of page with ribbon; string tag through and attach with colored brad. Journal on white textured cardstock; cut and mount. Stamp title on top of journaling box with letter stamps and lavender ink; layer with rub-on word. Stamp remainder of journaling on bottom of journaling box with lavender ink.

*Alison Chabe, Charleston, Massachusetts*
*Photo: Matthew Chabe, Charleston, Massachusetts*

**SUPPLIES:** Lavender linen cardstock, patterned papers, molding strips, paper tag, rub-on word (Chatterbox); letter stamps (FontWerks, Hero Arts); white textured cardstock (Bazzill); ribbon; lavender and black inks; colored brad

## Tooth Fairy
### INCORPORATE INTERNET FONTS

A fancy title font and journaling printed on an oversized photo mat make Michon's journaling visually appealing. Turn a patterned paper background sideways. Journal on blue cardstock; cut out, leaving room for photo. Adhere photo and mat onto green cardstock; mount on page. Print title and remainder of journaling on pink cardstock; cut out and mat on green cardstock. Mat secondary photo on blue cardstock; mount on page along with matted title block. Affix flower jewel in center of metal flower charm; mount onto title box.

*Michon Kessler, Alturas, California*

**SUPPLIES:** Patterned paper (KI Memories); metal flower charm (Making Memories); green, blue and pink cardstocks; flower jewel

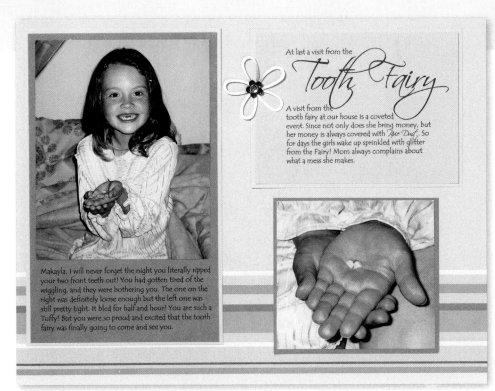

At last a visit from the *Tooth Fairy*

A visit from the tooth fairy at our house is a coveted event. Since not only does she bring money, but her money is always covered with *Pixie Dust*, so for days the girls wake up sprinkled with glitter from the Fairy! Mom always complains about what a mess she makes.

Makayla, I will never forget the night you literally ripped your two front teeth out! You had gotten tired of the wiggling, and they were bothering you. The one on the right was definitely loose enough but the left one was still pretty tight. It bled for half and hour! You are such a Tuffy! But you were so proud and excited that the tooth fairy was finally going to come and see you.

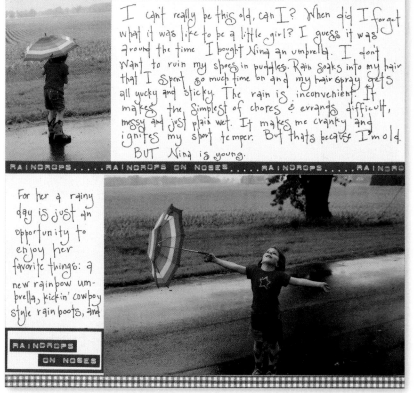

For her a rainy day is just an opportunity to enjoy her favorite things: a new rainbow umbrella, kickin' cowboy style rain boots, and

## Raindrops On Noses

### WRITE BLOCK-STYLE ON A BACKGROUND

Elizabeth used cater-cornered journaling blocks written directly on her page to contrast how the rain makes her feel as an adult compared to how her daughter feels about it as a child. Adhere photos on a pale yellow textured cardstock background. Affix gingham ribbon across top and bottom of page. Adhere label across center of page. Apply label title onto red cardstock-mounted rectangle; adhere. Journal in open spaces in black pen.

*Elizabeth Ruuska, Rensselaer, Indiana*

**SUPPLIES:** Pale yellow textured cardstock (Bazzill); labels (Dymo); gingham ribbon; red cardstock; black pen

## Shades of Davi

### INCORPORATE DESCRIPTIVE PAINT CHIPS

Johanna strategically employed paint chips with descriptive names to portray her daughter's persona. Mat white cardstock on a light green textured cardstock background; machine stitch. Apply rub-on letters to photo and adhere. Stamp title with foam stamps using orange and green paints. Cut out and mount paint chips, covering white cardstock section. Attach silk flowers with large colored brads.

*Johanna Peterson, El Cajon, California*

**SUPPLIES:** Light green textured cardstock (Bazzill); rub-on letters, foam stamps, silk flowers, large colored brads (Making Memories); white cardstock; orange and green paints; paint chips

## ...Favorite Things

### FRAME JOURNALING WITH BLOCK PATTERNS

Block-patterned paper provided perfect compartments for Megan's handwritten journaling in which she documents her daughter's current favorites. Crop color and sepia photos; adhere in select blocks of patterned paper background. Assemble collage for center square using inked paper square adorned with smaller handwritten square and torn and cut paper strips. Handwrite title, wrap block with fiber and mount. Punch two holes along side of block, thread with pink ribbon and tie. Fill remaining blocks with handwritten journaling and accent with stickers, torn paper elements, metal letters and brads.

*Megan Jones, Spring, Texas*

**SUPPLIES:** Patterned papers (Paper Adventures, Paper Illuzionz, Rusty Pickle); metal-rimmed tag, metal letters (Making Memories); letter stickers (Li'l Davis Designs); brads, ribbon; pen

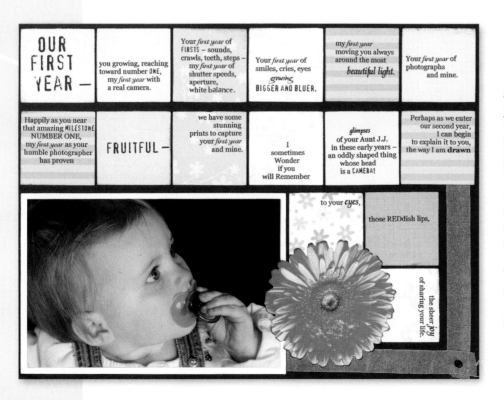

## Our First Year

### JOURNAL IN CROPPED PAPER BLOCKS

J.J. summarized in journaling boxes the firsts that she and her daughter shared together in the twelve months following her birth. Turn an 8½ x 11" black cardstock background sideways. Adhere ribbon down right side and across bottom; attach brad at intersection. Mat photo on white cardstock; adhere on bottom left corner. Print title and journaling on various patterned papers; punch into squares, ink edges in black and mount around photo. Ink edges of flower die cut and adhere.

*J.J. Killins, Redondo Beach, California*

**SUPPLIES:** Patterned paper (Chatterbox); flower die cut (Colorbök); black and white cardstocks; ribbon; brad; black ink

## Nothing's Going to Stop Me
### INCORPORATE SONG LYRICS

Felicia is reminded of her daughter every time she hears a particular song, so she included lyric excerpts in her journaling. Cut two different patterned paper strips; ink edges in brown and staple along top and bottom of pink patterned paper background. Mat photo on blue cardstock; tear edges and attach with brads. Using foam letter stamps and purple paint, stamp portion of title along bottom of page. Use rub-on letters for remainder of title. Stamp flowers on bottom of page, using eyelets for flower centers. Adhere acrylic charm over "O" in title. Print journaling on a transparency; cut out and staple to page. Stitch patterned paper block on blue cardstock mat and ink edges in brown; embellish with acrylic baubles and attach with brads. Apply rub-on letters next to square element for portion of journaling. Paint letter stencil and flower clip purple; once dry, adhere stencil over white cardstock and mount on photo. Affix flower clip over brad on photo. Handwrite date next to picture.

*Felicia Krelwitz, Lake Zurich, Illinois*

**SUPPLIES:** Patterned papers, flower die cut and acrylic letter cubes (KI Memories); foam letter stamps (Making Memories); rub-on letters (Chatterbox, Making Memories); flower stamp (source unknown); acrylic charm (Doodlebug Design); letter stencil (www.Scrapaddict.com); flower clip (Scrapworks); stapler; brown ink; blue cardstock; brads; purple paint; transparency

## Tell Me...
### INCLUDE A PLAYFUL POEM

A fun verse by Shel Silverstein helped Maria say in her journaling how she feels about her daughter. Cut strip of green cardstock; layer onto a white cardstock background. Journal on bottom left corner of orange textured cardstock section; mount on background. Cut patterned paper section; tear corner to reveal journaling beneath and adhere. Print photo with white border; cut out and mount. Accent with buttons. Cut three lengths of paper yarn; knot and affix on upper right corner of page.

*Maria Newport, Smyrna, Georgia*

**SUPPLIES:** Orange textured cardstock (Bazzill); patterned paper (SEI); paper yarn (Emagination Crafts); green and white cardstocks; buttons

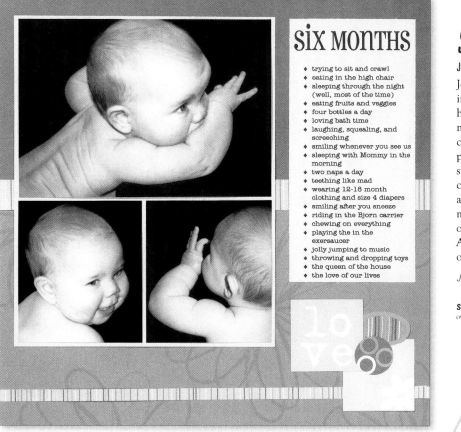

## SIX MONTHS

- trying to sit and crawl
- eating in the high chair
- sleeping through the night (well, most of the time)
- eating fruits and veggies
- four bottles a day
- loving bath time
- laughing, squealing, and screeching
- smiling whenever you see us
- sleeping with Mommy in the morning
- two naps a day
- teething like mad
- wearing 12-18 month clothing and size 4 diapers
- smiling after you sneeze
- riding in the Bjorn carrier
- chewing on everything
- playing the in the exersaucer
- jolly jumping to music
- throwing and dropping toys
- the queen of the house
- the love of our lives

## Six Months

### JOURNAL MILESTONES WITH A BULLETED LIST

Jess used a bulleted list for a quick and informative means of documenting her daughter's accomplishments at six months. Cut a large section of brown cardstock; layer over flower patterned paper background. Cut two strips of striped patterned paper; mount across center and bottom of background. Mat all photos on single pink cardstock mat; mount on page. Create a bulleted list on pink cardstock; cut out and adhere. Assemble punch-out squares, circle and oval onto bottom right corner of page.

*Jess Atkinson, Harrisburg, Pennsylvania*

**SUPPLIES:** Patterned papers, punch-out squares, circle and oval (KI Memories); pink cardstock

## Sophie's Milestones

### SHOWCASE ACHIEVEMENTS WITH TAGS

Debbie used tags to sum up this little girl's first year milestones. Mat striped patterned paper on tan cardstock background. Create pocket by cutting square from polka-dot patterned paper; mat on tan cardstock, applying adhesive to bottom and side edges only. Affix self-adhesive zipper on top edge; mount piece on page. Attach charm hung from pink jump rings to zipper pull. Double mat photo on pink and tan cardstocks; mount slightly over pocket. Cut strip of square patterned paper; mat on tan cardstock and adhere. Affix die-cut letters for portion of title onto strip. Complete title by stitching pink letter buttons on bottom of page. Journal onto white cardstock; cut into tags and mat on tan cardstock. Punch holes in tops of tags, tie with fibers and slide into pocket.

*Debbie Hill, Westford, Massachusetts*
*Photo: Jennifer Frank, Peoria, Arizona*

**SUPPLIES:** Patterned papers (Stampin' Up!); self-adhesive zipper, pink jump rings, charm, letter buttons (Junkitz); die-cut letters (QuicKutz); tan, pink and white cardstocks; hole punch; fibers

## You at Almost 2

### INCLUDE MATCHBOOK-STYLE JOURNALING STRIPS

Rhonda created folded journaling strip accents modeled after matchbooks that open to reveal additional journaling. Turn tan cardstock background sideways. Layer cut sections of patterned paper, green textured cardstock and olive cardstock onto page along with photo. Replace center of metal-rimmed tag with circle punched from olive cardstock; mount. Fold and staple small piece of patterned paper and mount on top of tag. Apply title using various letter stickers. Cut strips from olive cardstock; fold left edges over and staple. Fold right side over so right edge tucks into stapled piece on each. Stamp journaling onto top of strip; open up and journal inside. Mount all onto page. Stamp date on upper left corner of page.

*Rhonda Bonifay, Virginia Beach, Virginia*

**SUPPLIES:** Patterned paper (Anna Griffin); green textured cardstock (Bazzill); various letter stickers (Creative Imaginations, Me & My Big Ideas); letter stamps (PSX Design); date stamp (Making Memories); tan and olive cardstocks; circle metal-rimmed tag; circle punch; stapler

## Xander The Stander

### JOURNAL IN VERTICAL STRIPS

Vertically mounted journaling strips that span the page cleverly parallel the story of April's son's love of standing on his own two feet. Ink edges of green patterned paper background in brown. Mat enlarged photo on brown textured cardstock and adhere. Print title on pink cardstock; cut, ink edges and mount vertically. Journal on yellow cardstock; cut into strips, ink edges and mount vertically on page between photo and title.

*April Peterson, Sacramento, California*

**SUPPLIES:** Patterned paper (SEI); brown textured cardstock (Bazzill); pink and yellow cardstocks; brown ink

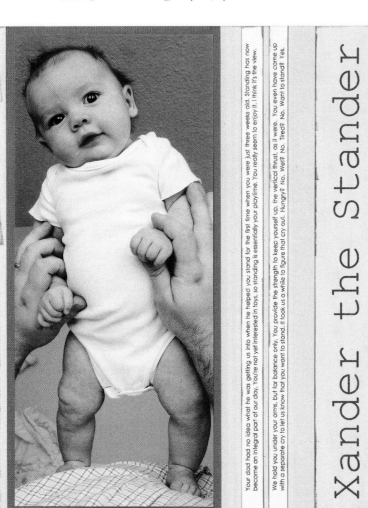

## Poki

### "ADVERTISE" ENDEARING QUALITIES

Stephanie cleverly described her new puppy by journaling all his endearing quirks and characteristics in a classified ad format. Make a copy of your local classified ads on white cardstock. Tear and mat on black cardstock background. Cut four thin strips of red cardstock and mount on page edges to frame. Double mat photos on red and white cardstocks; adhere. Colorize metal phrase eyelets and letters with silver leafing pen; mat letters on red cardstock and adhere on page. Mount word eyelets on "ad" and on both photos. Journal in classified ad style on white cardstock; double mat on black and red cardstocks and mount with foam adhesive. Accent top corner of page with paper clip.

*Stephanie Milner, Ventura, California*

**SUPPLIES:** Metal phrase eyelets and letter charms (Making Memories); silver leafing pen (Krylon); classified ads; white, black and red cardstocks; paper clip

## Such a Boy

### COMBINE CHARACTERISTICS WITH BITS OF DIALOGUE

Jess endearingly detailed her son's personality by stringing together characteristics and silly quotes, putting his exact words in italics. Cut sections of white cardstock and striped patterned paper; detail edges with black pen and layer over navy blue cardstock background. Journal on white cardstock; cut, edge with black pen and adorn with die cuts. Mount piece on page. Mat photo on orange textured cardstock; layer on oversized teal cardstock block, add pen detail and mount. Apply various letter stickers for title. Adhere punch-out square next to photo mat; stamp letter with foam letter stamp in orange ink. Outline in black pen. Embellish square with metal stencil letter.

*Jess Atkinson, Harrisburg, Pennsylvania*

**SUPPLIES:** Patterned paper, die cuts, punch-out square (KI Memories); orange textured cardstock (Bazzill); letter stickers (KI Memories, Sticker Studio); foam letter stamp (Making Memories); metal stencil letter (Colorbök); white, purple and green cardstocks; black pen; orange ink

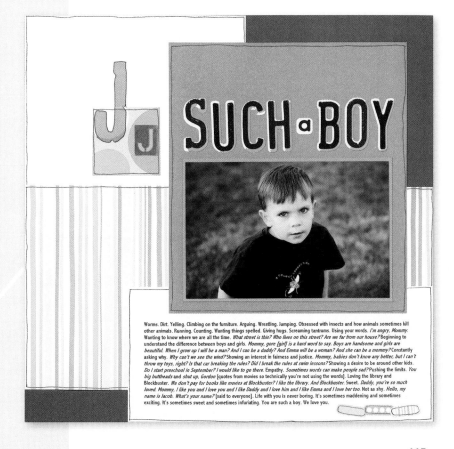

## Let's Talk
### RECOUNT FUNNY DIALOGUE

Susan creatively captured some of her son's favorite words to help remember a fun fragment of time forever. Using image-editing software, create background by applying title and journaling; lighten a portion of your text to simulate vellum and add text. Print and mount photo.

*Susan Cyrus, Broken Arrow, Oklahoma*

**SUPPLIES:** Image-editing software (Adobe); white cardstock

It's finally happening Connor: you're actually starting to talk! All this time with so little progress, and now you're suddenly quite a chatterbox! Your favorite word is still "no," and you're likely to call any and every color "white," but I don't care. We've got a lot of catching up to do!

Me: Can you say purple?
You: Puh-ple?
Me: Can you say blue?
You: Booo ...
Me: Can you say PaPa?
You: Pa Pa?
Me: Can you say Grannie?
You: Nah-nee?

Me: Can you say duck?
You: (Giggles) Duck ... duck ... duck ...
Me: Can you say dog?
You: Duck?
Me: Can you say red?
You: White.

February 2004

---

There is a Japanese restaurant that has a small **water wheel** in front of it's parking lot right by the road. We drive by it every time we go to Costco or Home Depot. Sometimes it is turning and sometimes it is not.

"Mommy, **why** isn't the water wheel turning?", he asked one day.

"Umm, I don't know", I said, as I sat there in traffic. I was trying to think of **reasons** it would be off. Maybe to save water or energy? There must be some underlying reason for the water wheel to be turned off. Maybe the restaurant only turns it on when it opens for dinner? I didn't know. How do you explain that to a 3 year old?

As I thought about my possible answers to his question, I finally said, **"I don't know, David,** why do you think the water wheel isn't running?" (I was obviously taking the easy way out!)

David had the most logical, intelligent answer to his seemingly complex question:

**"Because somebody turned it off!"**

## Intelligence
### JOURNAL A CONVERSATION

Mimi captured a conversation with her son that she can smile back on for years to come. Journal on a blue textured cardstock background. Layer right side with black textured cardstock. Add photo. Cut patterned paper strip; affix across page. Stamp title across bottom of page with foam stamps using black ink on blue cardstock background and white ink on black cardstock background.

*Mimi Schramm, Colton, California*

**SUPPLIES:** Blue and black textured cardstocks (DieCuts with a View); patterned paper (Colorbök); foam stamps (Making Memories); black and white inks

INTELLIGENCE

## ...I've Got a Snake in My Boot

### JOURNAL WITH LABELS

Here a label maker puts a fun twist on telling a story. Begin with two yellow textured cardstock backgrounds. Layer with torn and rolled textured black cardstock and torn patterned paper. Add textured red and yellow cardstock strips to tops and bottoms of pages. Sand bandanna border stickers and affix along bottoms of pages. On left page, triple mat photo on red, white and black textured cardstocks; adhere on page. Accent with yellow textured cardstock squares; ink in black and attach with decorative brads. Ink edges of library card; add photo corners and label journaling; mount over ribbon attached with decorative brad. On right page, double mat photos on white and red textured cardstocks; mount. Punch squares for portion of title; ink in black and mount along bottoms of both pages. Apply letter acrylic word, stickers and labels to both pages for title. Embellish with square brads. Stamp date on top right corner of right page.

*Shelley Anderson, Plymouth, Minnesota*

**SUPPLIES:** Textured yellow, black, red and white cardstocks (Bazzill); bandanna border stickers (Mrs. Grossman's); patterned paper (Keeping Memories Alive); decorative brads, square brads (Making Memories); library card (www.scrapsahoy.com); photo corners (Canson); labels (Dymo); letter stickers (Creative Imaginations); acrylic word (Li'l Davis Designs); sandpaper; black ink; gingham ribbon; square punch

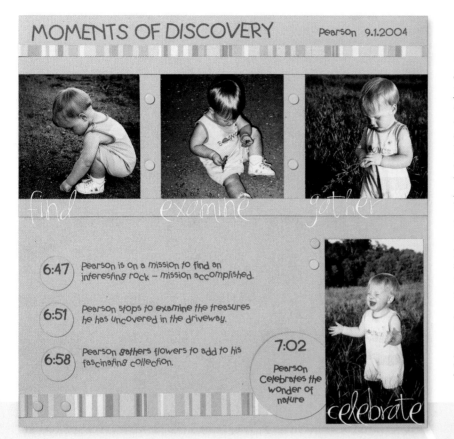

## Moments of Discovery
### JOURNAL A TIMELINE

Jodi employed timeline journaling to chronicle her little one's activities in endearing detail. Print title and journaling on a blue textured cardstock background. Mount cropped photos along top; set two colored brads between each photo. Flank with strips of green textured cardstock. Add patterned paper strips along top and bottom of page; accent with brads. Apply rub-on words below photos. Print time information on green textured cardstock; punch into circles and mount on page along with remaining photo. Attach two more colored brads near top of photo and rub-on word on bottom of photo.

*Jodi Heinen, Sartell, Minnesota*
*Photos: Cathy Kuchinski, Holdingford, Minnesota*

**SUPPLIES:** Blue and green textured cardstocks (Bazzill); patterned paper (Daisy D's); rub-on words (Making Memories); colored brads; circle punch

## My Husband
### SUMMARIZE A LOVED ONE'S ACHIEVEMENTS TO-DATE

Cheryl commemorated what she has admired about her husband in the years they have been together with a heartfelt list. Print title on olive patterned paper; cut out and mount atop brown cardstock background. Cut section of floral patterned paper and smaller section of striped patterned paper; layer both over background. Mat photo on brown cardstock and affix on page. Journal on brown patterned paper; cut, mat on brown cardstock and adhere. Affix expression ribbon across page along edges of patterned paper. Mat cropped photo on brown cardstock and adhere along with metal heart charm. Attach brads at all four corners of page.

*Cheryl Kolar, Gurnee, Illinois*

**SUPPLIES:** Olive, floral, striped and brown patterned papers (Chatterbox); expression ribbon, metal heart charm (Making Memories); brown cardstock; brads

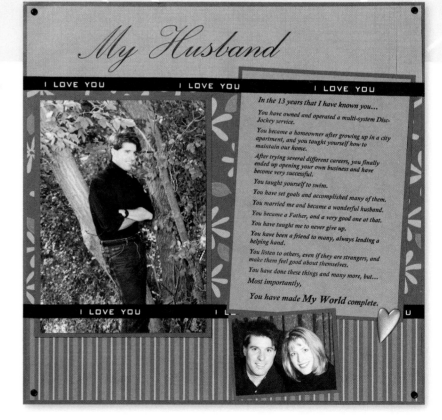

## *Magic*

### INCORPORATE SELECT CUT-OUT WORDS

By printing select words on contrasting-colored paper and in a slightly larger font, Angelia emphasized specific words in her journaling and also added visual interest. Layer brown patterned paper background with torn flower patterned paper. Journal on red linen patterned paper, making sure to accommodate highlighted words. Tear out and mount on bottom of page. Print select words onto tan cardstock; cut out, enhance with metallic rub-ons and mount on journaling box. Adhere two cut-out squares on sides of journaling box; attach hinges on each square with brads. Mat one photo on red linen patterned paper with photo corners; mount with unmatted photos. Stamp title on cut-out with letter stamps. Tie twine on each end of label holder and mount over title; secure on back of page.

*Angelia Wiggington, Belmont, Mississippi*

**SUPPLIES:** Patterned papers (Chatterbox, Daisy D's); metallic rub-ons (Craf-T); cut-outs (EK Success); hinges, label holder (Making Memories); photo corners (Canson); white cardstock; twine

## *Big Bowls*

### DRESS UP JOURNALING WITH AN IMAGE

Laura easily added visual interest to her journaling passage by printing and cutting out a dog bowl image from an Internet Web Site. Print title and journaling on lower half of gray cardstock background. Mat photos side by side on burgundy cardstock mat and mount at top of page. Print image of bowl; cut and affix on bottom right corner of page.

*Laura McGrover, Clearwater, Florida*

**SUPPLIES:** Gray and burgundy cardstocks

## Dare to Dream

### PAINT TRANSPARENCY-PRINTED JOURNALING

Acrylic paint applied to a transparency helped to highlight Suzy's insightful journaling. Sand red cardstock background. Tear section of patterned paper; sand, ink torn edge in black and mount. Sand section of metal sheet. Apply rub-on letters for portion of title; stamp remainder with foam letter stamps. Mount piece on page, adhering woven labels under right side. Ink measuring tape segment in black; accent with spiral clip. Journal on transparency; cut and paint on back with white acrylic paint. Once dry, mount on page. Mount photo; add pen outline. Sand metal photo corners and mount on right corners of page. Add decorative clip to left side of page.

*Suzy West, Fremont, California*

**SUPPLIES:** Patterned paper (Mustard Moon); metal sheet, rub-on letters, foam letter stamps, metal photo corners, spiral clip, decorative clip (Making Memories); woven labels, measuring tape (Me & My Big Ideas); red cardstock; sandpaper; black ink; black and white acrylic paints; black pen

## Wish

### COMBINE PRINTED TRANSPARENCIES

Sharon combined her transparency-printed journaling with sections cut from preprinted transparencies to flank a special photo. Mat patterned paper on a black textured cardstock background. Cut squares of equal size from patterned paper and black and brown textured cardstocks; mat all together on black textured cardstock mat, then mount onto page. Cut preprinted transparencies to fit black square cardstock pieces. Print journaling on transparency, leaving room for photo; cut and mount over brown textured cardstock section. Ink photo edges in black and adhere. Adorn corners with metal charms. Wrap ribbon around top of page and tie. Apply title acrylic letter charms to ribbon for title and date with acrylic number charms.

*Sharon Laakkonen, Superior, Wisconsin*

**SUPPLIES:** Patterned paper (7 Gypsies, Rusty Pickle); black and brown textured cardstocks (Bazzill); preprinted transparencies (Scrapping With Style); metal charms (Card Connection); acrylic letter and number charms (K & Company); transparency; black ink; ribbon

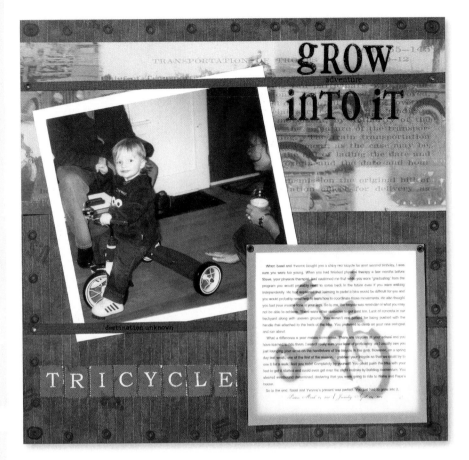

## Grow Into It

### ENHANCE VELLUM JOURNALING WITH A DIE CUT

Debra emphasized her page theme by adding a die cut underneath her vellum journaling. Cut brown patterned paper section and adhere along top of blue patterned paper background. Use image-editing software to colorize the bike in the black-and-white photo; print with white border and mount. Cut thin strips of red textured cardstock; attach along top and bottom of page with eyelets. Embellish strips with rub-on phrases. Apply title with letter stickers. Tear out perforated letters from paper and mount. Adhere tricycle die-cut on white cardstock square; mat on black textured cardstock. Journal on vellum and cut to fit mat; attach with eyelets. Mount with foam adhesive.

*Debra Hendren, Royal Oak, Michigan*

**SUPPLIES:** Patterned papers (Karen Foster Design, Rusty Pickle); red textured cardstock (Bazzill); rub-on phrases (Making Memories); letter stickers (Me & My Big Ideas); tricycle die cut (EK Success); image-editing software (Adobe Photoshop); eyelets; white and black cardstocks; vellum; foam adhesive

## The Difference a Day Can Make

### CREATE A JOURNALING OVERLAY

April conveyed how her baby changed her life overnight by printing her reflective journaling on a transparency to form an overlay. Cut section from white textured cardstock and ink in green; mount on a green textured cardstock background. Turn page sideways and mount photo. Journal onto transparency; cut and mount over photo. Affix gingham ribbon along seams of papers.

*April Peterson, Sacramento, California*
*Photo: Steven Peterson, Sacramento, California*

**SUPPLIES:** White and green textured cardstocks (Bazzill); green ink; transparency; gingham ribbon

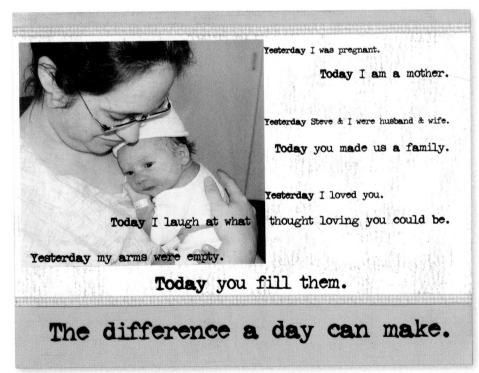

# Constant Companion

## ENHANCE JOURNALING USING YOUR COMPUTER

Design elements created using computer software helped to add an artistic element to showcase tender journaling. Begin with two green textured cardstock backgrounds. Using a word processing program, create journaling circles, journaling and title; print onto both pages and red cardstock. For left page, mat photo on red cardstock, tear off bottom edge and mount. Adhere "S" element printed on red cardstock. For right page, mat enlarged photo on pink and black textured cardstocks; mount. Tear corner piece from red cardstock and apply stamped caption.

*Karen Wilson-Bonner, Pleasanton, California*

**SUPPLIES:** Green, pink and black textured cardstocks (Bazzill); word processing program (Microsoft); letter stamps (Hero Arts); red cardstock

## *Letters to My Brothers*

### HOUSE JOURNALING CARDS IN A POCKET

Giovanna created pull-out cards to feature letters to each of her brothers. Begin with two patterned paper backgrounds. On left page, cut section for pocket from blue cardstock. Cut strip from patterned paper, tearing off bottom edge; machine stitch across top of cardstock piece. Attach to page with eyelets. Using a word processing program, create a text box to arrange title in the form of a frame around the enlarged photo; print onto green cardstock, cut out and add photo. Mount onto pocket. Tear corner from blue cardstock and adhere on bottom right corner of pocket; embellish with dimensional stickers. Write letters on taupe cardstock, cut into cards and top with cut sections of green cardstock. Add metal eyelet words; slip cards into pocket. For right page, mat photos on long sections of green cardstock; tear off one end of each. Layer over photos, machine stitch and add to page. Attach vellum metal-rimmed tags with eyelets; handwrite names. Attach eyelet phrase.

*Giovanna Thompson, Erie, Pennsylvania*
*Photos: Katherine Majalca, Green Valley, Arizona*

**SUPPLIES:** Patterned papers (Robin's Nest); metal eyelet words, metal eyelet phrase, vellum metal-rimmed tags (Making Memories); word processing program (Microsoft); blue, green and taupe cardstocks; eyelets

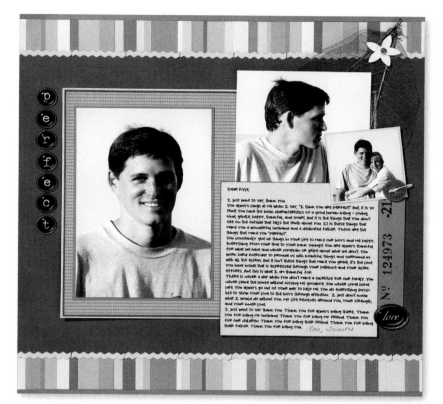

## Perfect

### WRITE A LETTER TO YOUR SPOUSE

Holly composed a love letter of thanks detailing what she appreciates most about her husband. Cut two patterned paper strips, two thin strips of blue cardstock, and rickrack-style die-cut strips from yellow textured cardstock. Mount along top and bottom of sienna textured cardstock background. Add skeleton leaves along flower accent made with a brad and photo turns. Mat focal photo on blue textured cardstock. Double mat on sienna and yellow textured cardstocks; mount. Journal on olive textured cardstock; cut, ink edges in black and mount. Add cropped unmatted photo. Mount journaling on page over preprinted tag. Mat small photo on olive textured cardstock. Attach washer word on corner of photo with safety pin; mount piece on page. Affix letter pebbles down left side of page for title. Adorn corner of tag with word pebble.

*Holly Corbett, Central, South Carolina*

**SUPPLIES:** Patterned papers (Chatterbox); sienna, yellow and blue textured cardstocks (Bazzill); rickrack die-cuts (QuicKutz); photo turns, washer word (Making Memories); preprinted tag (EK Success); letter and word pebble (Li'l Davis Designs); skeleton leaves; brads; black ink; safety pin

## Love Notes

### FEATURE LOVE NOTES

Melanie mused in this layout on the little love notes she finds in her luggage from her family while away from home, and included examples. Ink the inside edges of precut window openings of background page in black; adhere love notes under openings. Cut patterned paper strips to flank both sides of openings. Journal directly onto page. Using computer font as guide, cut portion of title from black textured cardstock; mount. Stamp remainder of title in green onto patterned paper with letter stamps; cut each letter and mount. Add labels to top and bottom of page. Ink metal frame in green and cover with clear embossing powder; heat to set. Tie black ribbon around frame, hanging mini tag containing date. Mount frame at askew angle over center note.

*Melanie Bauer, Columbia, Missouri*

**SUPPLIES:** Background paper, patterned paper, metal frame (Making Memories); black patterned paper (Chatterbox); textured cardstock (Bazzill); letter stamps (Ma Vinci's Reliquary); labels (Dymo); black and green inks; ribbon; mini tag; embossing powder

## ...Happily Ever After
### EMPLOY DEFINITIONS FOR JOURNALING

Katrina used definitions of wedding elements for a fun turn on her journaling. Cut sections from black textured cardstock and mount on mauve textured cardstock background. Print definitions on floral patterned paper; mount. Mat enlarged photo on black textured cardstock mat; tear bottom edge. Wrap preprinted ribbon around top of photo and gingham ribbon around bottom; adhere to page. Mount fabric label title on photo. Print caption on vellum; punch with circle punch to fit metal-rimmed tag; tie with gingham ribbon, mat on black textured cardstock and adhere above journaling. Affix preprinted ribbon below journaling and rub-on words on top left and bottom right corners of page. Affix metal label holder over rub-on word on bottom corner with brads.

*Katrina Hogan, Weatherford, Texas*

**SUPPLIES:** Black and mauve textured cardstocks (Bazzill); floral patterned paper (Anna Griffin); preprinted ribbon, fabric label (Making Memories); metal label holder (EK Success); gingham ribbon; vellum, metal-rimmed tag; brads

## Bloom
### WRITE YOUR OWN "DEFINITION"

Here Kimberly employed the fun and simple technique of acrostic journaling, which uses each letter of a word to begin a sentence. Place inked yellow and pink textured cardstocks and orange cardstock circles on a green textured cardstock background. Cut patterned paper section; adhere. Cut cover from flower greeting card; ink edges and mount. Affix mesh across bottom of page; layer with photo. Punch holes on either side of flower stem, thread ribbon through and tie. Punch small circles from pink, green and yellow textured cardstocks and orange cardstock; stamp title on circles and mount on card. Print journaling and photo caption onto transparency; cut and affix journaling with clock hand and brad and adhere caption to photo.

*Kimberly Kesti, Phoenix, Arizona*

**SUPPLIES:** Pink, yellow and green textured cardstocks (Bazzill); patterned paper (Li'l Davis Designs); flower greeting card (Hallmark); mesh (Magenta); letter stamps (Memory Lane); clock hand (Ink It!); black ink; orange cardstock; ribbon; transparency; brad

# Additional Credits and Sources

**Cover**
*Jodi Amidei, Memory Makers Books*

**SUPPLIES:** Orange textured cardstock (Crafter's Workshop); patterned paper (Stampin' Up!); self-adhesive index tabs (Z International); red and yellow cardstocks; black ink; bandanna fabric; yellow floss; foam adhesive; large and mini square punches

**p.3 Bookplate**
*Jodi Amidei, Memory Makers Books*

**SUPPLIES:** Patterned paper (Stampin' Up!); punches (Emagination Crafts, Family Treasures); red and yellow cardstocks; bandanna fabric; black chalk ink; yellow embroidery thread

**p.6 Cruise**
*Jodi Amidei, Memory Makers Books; Photos: Emily Curry Hitchingham, Memory Makers Books*

**SUPPLIES:** Patterned paper (NRN Designs); title (Sarah Heidt Photocraft); ribbon (source unknown); buckles (Junkitz); stickers (Paper House Productions); definition sticker (Daisy D's)

**p. 8** bag (Crop In Style) mat (C-Thru Ruler) paper trimmer (Fiskars) adhesives (American Tombow, Glue Dots) Scrap-A-Logs (Artfully Scribed) embellishment organizer (Advantus/Cropper Hopper) **p. 9** adhesive-application machine (Xyron) color wheel (Pick, Point &n Match) die-cutting machines and die cuts (Accu-Cut, QuicKutz, Sizzix) **p. 10** stickers and stamps (Destination Scrapbook Designs) **p. 11** coordinating papers and accents (Chatterbox) faux embellishments (Cloud 9 Design, EK Success, Leisure Arts, Sticker Studio, Tumblebeasts) premade accents (Autumn Leaves, Colorbök, EK Success, Memories Complete) **p. 12** pre-printed sentiments (Karen Foster Design, Making Memories, Memories Complete) quote books (Autumn Leaves, Chatterbox, DieCuts with a View)

**p. 14 Best Friends**
*Michelle Tornay, Newark, California*

**SUPPLIES:** Blue textured cardstock (Bazzill); patterned paper (KI Memories); letter stamps (All Night Media, PSX Design); watch crystal (Scrapworks); black ribbon; transparency

**p. 36 Braden**
*Nicola Howard, Pukekone, South Aukland, New Zealand*

**SUPPLIES:** Dark taupe, light taupe, light spruce and dark spruce textured cardstock backgrounds (Bazzill); striped patterned paper (Chatterbox); letter stamps (PSX Design); date stamp (Making Memories); black ink; letter stencil; twill tape

**p. 56 Challenges**
*Jodi Heinen, Sartell, Minnesota
Photo: Michael Ruehle, Andover, Minnesota*

**SUPPLIES:** Striped patterned paper (SEI); blue textured cardstock (Bazzill); metal mesh (Making Memories); letter die cuts (source unknown); snowflake laser cuts; snowflake charm (source unknown); brown cardstock; brown pen; metal rimmed circle tag; circle punch

**p. 80 Star Fish**
*Jessie Baldwin, Las Vegas, Nevada*

**SUPPLIES:** Dark brown and light brown textured cardstocks (Bazzill); fabric paper and fabric labels (Me & My Big Ideas); letter stickers (EK Success); light blue and sky blue cardstocks; brown ink; label holders; brads; starfish cut from napkin ring

**p. 108 Do You Dream in Color?**
*Kitty Foster, Snellville, Georgia*

**SUPPLIES:** Patterned papers and ribbon (SEI); "dream" word (Pressed Petals); transparency; ink

# Source guide

The following companies manufacture products featured in this book. Please check your local retailers to find these materials, or go to a company's Web site for the latest product. In addition, we have made every attempt to properly credit the items mentioned in this book. We apologize to any company that we have listed incorrectly, and we would appreciate hearing from you.

7 Gypsies
(800) 588-6707
www.7gypsies.com

Accu-Cut®
(800) 288-1670
www.accucut.com

Adobe
www.adobe.com

All Night Media- see Plaid Enterprises

American Art Clay Co. (AMACO)
(800) 374-1600
www.amaco.com

American Crafts
(801) 226-0747
www.americancrafts.com

American Tombow, Inc.
(800) 835-3232
www.tombowusa.com

American Traditional Designs®
(800) 448-6656
www.americantraditional.com

Anna Griffin, Inc.
(888) 817-8170
www.annagriffin.com

ArcSoft®
www.arcsoft.com

Artfully Scribed
(703) 78-STAMP
www.artfullyscribed.com

Artistic Expressions
(219) 764-5158
www.artisticexpressionsinc.com

Autumn Leaves
(800) 588-6707
www.autumnleaves.com

Avery Dennison Corporation
(800) GO-AVERY
www.avery.com

Basic Grey™
(801) 451-6006
www.basicgrey.com

Bazzill Basics Paper
(480) 558-8557
www.bazzillbasics.com

Beary Patch, The
(877) 327-2111
www.bearypatchinc.com

Blue Moon Beads
(800) 377-6715
www.bluemoonbeads.com

Bo-Bunny Press
(801) 771-4010
www.bobunny.com

Books By Hand- no contact info

Boutique Trims, Inc.
(248) 437-2017
www.boutiquetrims.com

Boxer Scrapbook Productions
(888) 625-6255
www.boxerscrapbooks.com

Canson®, Inc.
(800) 628-9283
www.canson-us.com

Card Connection- see Michaels

Carolee's Creations®
(435) 563-1100
www.ccpaper.com

Chatterbox, Inc.
(208) 939-9133
www.chatterboxinc.com

Chronicle Books
(800) 722-6656
www.chroniclebooks.com

Clearsnap, Inc.
(800) 448-4862
www.clearsnap.com

Close To My Heart®
(888) 655-6552
www.closetomyheart.com

Cloud 9 Design
(763) 493-0990
www.cloud9design.biz

Club Scrap™
(888) 634-9100
www.clubscrap.com

Colorbök™, Inc.
(800) 366-4660
www.colorbok.com

Corel Corporation
(800) 772-6735
www.corel.com

Craf-T Products
(507) 235-3996
www.craf-tproducts.com

Crafter's Workshop, The
(877) CRAFTER
www.thecraftersworkshop.com

Creative Imaginations
(800) 942-6487
www.cigift.com

Creative Impressions Rubber Stamps, Inc.
(719) 596-4860
www.creativeimpressions.com

Creative Memories®
(800) 468-9335
www.creativememories.com

Creative Paperclay Company®
(800) 484-6648
www.paperclay.com

Creek Bank Creations, Inc.
(217) 427-5980
www.creekbankcreations.com

Crop In Style®
(888) 700-2202
www.cropinstyle.com

Cropper Hopper™/ Advantus Corporation
(800) 826-8806
www.cropperhopper.com

C-Thru® Ruler Company, The
(800) 243-8419
www.cthruruler.com

Daisy D's Paper Company
(888) 601-8955
www.daisydspaper.com

Darice, Inc.
(800) 321-1494
www.darice.com

Deluxe Designs
(480) 205-9210
www.deluxedesigns.com

Design Originals
(800) 877-0067
www.d-originals.com

Destination™ Scrapbook Designs
(866) 806-7826
www.destinationstickers.com

DieCuts with a View™
(877) 221-6107
www.dcwv.com

DMD Industries, Inc.
(800) 805-9890
www.dmdind.com

Doodlebug Design™ Inc.
(801) 966-9952
www.doodlebugdesigninc.com

Duncan Enterprises
(800) 782-6748
www.duncancrafts.com

Dymo
www.dymo.com

EK Success™, Ltd.
(800) 524-1349
www.eksuccess.com

Emagination Crafts, Inc.
(630) 833-9521
www.emaginationcrafts.com

Embelleez
(516) 510-3286
www.embelleez.com

Family Treasures, Inc.®
www.familytreasures.com

Fiskars, Inc.
(800) 950-0203
www.fiskars.com

Flair® Designs
(888) 546-9990
www.flairdesignsinc.com

FontWerks
www.fontwerks.com

Frances Meyer
(413) 584-5446
www.francesmeyer.com

Glue Dots® International
(888) 688-7131
www.gluedots.com

Hallmark Cards, Inc.
(800) 425-6275
www.hallmark.com

Heidi Grace Designs
(866) 89-HEIDI
www.heidigrace.com

Hero Arts® Rubber Stamps, Inc.
(800) 822-4376
www.heroarts.com
Hollos Paper Supply- no contact info
Hot Off The Press, Inc.
(800) 227-9595
www.paperpizazz.com
Ink It!-no contact info
Itty Bitty Buckles- no contact info
Jacquard Products/Rupert, Gibbon &
Spider, Inc.
(800) 442-0455
www.jacquardproducts.com
Jest Charming
(702) 564-5101
www.jestcharming.com
Jo-Ann Stores
(888) 739-4120
www.joann.com
JudiKins
(310) 515-1115
www.judikins.com
Junkitz™
(732) 792-1108
www.junkitz.com
K & Company
(888) 244-2083
www.kandcompany.com
Karen Foster Design
(801) 451-9779
www.karenfosterdesign.com
Keeping Memories Alive™
(800) 419-4949
www.scrapbooks.com
KI Memories
(972) 243-5595
www.kimemories.com
Krylon®
(216) 566-200
www.krylon.com
La Pluma, Inc.
(615) 273-7367
www.debrabeagle.com
Leisure Arts, Inc.
(800) 643-8030
www.leisurearts.com
Lifetime Moments-no contact
info
Li'l Davis Designs
(949) 838-0344
www.lildavisdesigns.com
LuminArte
(866) 229-1544
www.luminarteinc.com
Magenta Rubber Stamps
(800) 565-5254
www.magentastyle.com
Magic Mesh
(651) 345-6374
www.magicmesh.com
Magic Scraps™
(972) 238-1838
www.magicscraps.com
Making Memories
(800) 286-5263
www.makingmemories.com
Marvy® Uchida/Uchida of America
Corp.
(800) 541-5877
www.uchida.com

Masterpiece® Studios
(800) 447-0219
www.masterpiecestudios.com
Ma Vinci's Reliquary
http://crafts.dm.net/mall/reliquary/
May Arts
(800) 442-3950
www.mayarts.com
McGill, Inc.
(800) 982-9884
www.mcgillinc.com
me & my BiG ideas®
(949) 883-2065
www.meandmybigideas.com
Memories Complete™, LLC
(866) 966-6365
www.memoriescomplete.com
Memory Lane-no contact info
Memory Stitches- no contact info
Michael Miller Memories
(212) 704-0774
www.michaelmillermemories.com
Michaels® Arts & Crafts
(800) 642-4235
www.michaels.com
Microsoft Corporation
www.microsoft.com
MoBe' Stamps!
(925) 443-2101
www.mobestamps.com
Mrs. Grossman's Paper Co.
(800) 429-4549
www.mrsgrossmans.com
Mustard Moon™
(408) 299-8542
www.mustardmoon.com
My Mind's Eye™, Inc.
(800) 665-5116
www.frame-ups.com
National Cardstock- no longer in business
NRN Designs
(800) 421-6958
www.nrndesigns.com
Nunn Design
(360) 379-3557
www.nunndesign.com
Offray
www.offray.com
Paper Adventures®
(800) 727-0699
www.paperadventures.com
Paper House Productions
(800) 255-7316
www.paperhouseproductions.com
Paper Illuzionz
(406) 234-8716
www.paperilluzionz.com
Paper Loft, The
(801) 254-1961
www.paperloft.com
Paper Source, The- no contact info
Papers by Catherine
(713) 723-3334
www.papersbycatherine.com
Papyrus- no contact info
Patchwork Paper Design, Inc.
(239) 481-4823
www.patchworkpaper.com

Pebbles Inc.
(801) 224-1857
www.pebblesinc.com
Photogenix- no contact info
Pioneer Photo Albums, Inc.®
(800) 366-3686
www.pioneerphotoalbums.com
Plaid Enterprises, Inc.
(800) 842-4197
www.plaidonline.com
Polaroid Corp.
(781) 386-2000
www.polaroid.com
Postmodern Design
(405) 321-3176
www.stampdiva.com
Pressed Petals
(800) 748-4656
www.pressedpetals.com
Provo Craft
(888) 577-3545
www.provocraft.com
PSX Design™
(800) 782-6748
www.psxdesign.com
QuicKutz
(801) 765-1144
www.quickutz.com
Ranger Industries, Inc.
(800) 244-2211
www.rangerink.com
River City Rubber Works
(800) 244-2211
www.rivercityrubberworks.com
Robin's Nest Press, The
(435) 789-5387
robins@sbnet.com
Rocky Mountain Scrapbook Co.
(801) 785-9695
www.rmscrapbook.com
Rubber Stampede
(800) 423-4135
www.deltacrafts.com
Rusty Pickle
(801) 272-2280
www.rustypickle.com
Sandylion Sticker Designs
(800) 387-4215
www.sandylion.com
Sarah Heidt Photo Craft LLC
(734) 424-2776
www.SarahHeidtPhotoCraft.com
Scenic Route Paper Co.
(801) 785-0761
www.scenicroutepaper.com
Scrap Ease®
(800) 272-3874
www.whatsnewltd.com
Scrapping With Style
(704) 254-6238
www.scrappingwithstyle.com
Scrappy Cat™, LLC
(440) 234-4850
www.scrappycatcreations.com
Scrapworks, LLC
(801) 363-1010
www.scrapworks.com
SEI, Inc.
(800) 333-3279
www.shopsei.com

Sizzix®
(866) 742-4447
www.sizzix.com
Staedtler®, Inc.
(800) 927-7723
www.staedtler.com
Stampabilities®
(800) 888-0321
www.stampabilities.com
Stampendous!®
(800) 869-0474
www.stampendous.com
Stampin' Up!®
(800) 782-6787
www.stampinup.com
Staples, Inc.
(800) 3-STAPLE
www.staples.com
Sticker Studio™
(208) 322-2465
www.stickerstudio.com
Sweetwater
(800) 359-3094
www.sweetwaterscrapbook.com
Therm O Web, Inc.
(800) 323-0799
www.thermoweb.com
Tsukineko®, Inc.
(800) 769-6633
www.tsukineko.com
Tumblebeasts LLC
(505) 323-5554
www.tumblebeasts.com
Two Busy Moms-see Deluxe
Designs
USArtQuest, Inc.
(517) 522-6225
www.usartquest.com
Vintage Workshop™ LLC, The
(913) 341-5559
www.thevintageworkshop.com
Wal-Mart Stores, Inc.
(800) WALMART
www.walmart.com
WBP Hamburg-no contact info
Westrim® Crafts
(800) 727-2727
www.westrimcrafts.com
Wordsworth
(719) 282-3495
www.wordsworthstamps.com
Wrights® Ribbon Accents
(877) 597-4448
www.wrights.com
Xyron, a division of Esselte
Corporation
(800) 793-3523
www.xyron.com
Z International-no contact info

# Index